KU-432-456

Traditional Recipes
using Olive Oil

The Best
of Spanish
and
Mediterranean
Cuisine

OLIVE OIL

The Spanish word for oil, *aceite*, comes from the Arabic **ZAIT AL-ZAITUM**, which means "juice of the olive". As such, the only true oil is that from olives. Others would merely be edible vegetable fat.

Research into olive cultivation suggests its origin dates as far back as 6000 BC, with the first plantations in present-day Libya, Israel and Syria.

The oldest known document on olive oil is from 2500 BC. Written on earthenware tablets, it tells of the importance of olive oil for the economy of CRETE during the reign of King Minos. An historical document, it makes the first known reference to the connection between olive oil and good health and to its dietary properties.

Even in ancient times, olive oil was highly regarded and seen as a basic foodstuff. Its versatility even led it to be considered sacred.

The Bible contains 140 mentions of olive oil and around 100 of the olive tree.

"And the dove came in to him in the evening; and, lo, in her mouth was an olive leaf pluckt off: so Noah knew that the waters were abated from off the earth." (Genesis, 8: 11)

"And thou shalt command the children of Israel, that they bring thee pure olive oil beaten for the light, to cause the lamp to burn always." (Exodus, 27: 20)

The first references to olive oil in Spain date back to the Roman Empire.

Hispania was the main supplier of olive oil to Rome, exporting it in sealed amphorae.

In 1878, a German archaeologist in Rome discovered Mount Testaccio, a hillock measuring 30 metres in height, on the bank of the river Tiber. It was made up of fragments of oil amphorae which had been stored there periodically over a century.

The shape of these amphorae and the lettering on their seals, SAGUNTUN, ITALICA, ASTIGI and CORDUBA, made it clear that they were of Spanish origin.

The Arab conquest of Spain at the beginning of the 8th century gave new impetus to the cultivation of olive trees, and olive oil was highly appreciated by the Muslims. It was a sign of identity for the Jews, who used it to trade and would buy all the oil produced in the special oil presses known as *almazaras*.

Together with the other two staple foods of the Mediterranean trilogy, bread and wine, olive oil required a special treatment process.

The importance of these basic foodstuffs led to the development of complex techniques for extraction, pressing, decanting, filtering and storage.

These techniques have, of course, advanced over the years, improving production and quality. We can now buy olive oils of exceptional quality which are becoming ever more available on the market.

Olive oil is still obtained by means of a physical process which fully respects the ancestral principles which have always been followed in the production of olive oil.

The olives must first mature, a slow process, during which the oil and other minor products are formed inside the olive, giving it that unmistakable aroma and taste.

Once the olives have reached their optimum maturity, they are then harvested by the traditional method of beating the branches with long poles, though in modern plantations mechanical vibrating machines are now used to loosen the olives from the branches.

With the utmost care so as not to damage the olives, they are then transferred to the presses, where they are processed immediately in order to avoid being stored in large piles for any length of time. They are only washed or winnowed to eliminate any earth or leaves.

The mass of pressed olives is placed into horizontal centrifuges or decanters, where the virgin olive oil is separated from the water and the leftover refuse of the fruit, known in Spanish as *orujo graso*.

This *orujo*, or refuse, which is particularly rich in antioxidants, proteins, sugars and mineral salts, is transferred to centres where it is recovered for later use.

We are thus left with the virgin olive oil, which must be treated and stored with great care to maintain its renowned natural organoleptic qualities. It is stored in stainless steel vats in air-conditioned cellars to maintain a constant temperature.

It is important to understand how olive oil is categorised, as there are many factors which can affect its quality, such as weather, plagues, early/late harvesting, faulty processing, incorrect storage, etc.

European Union regulations now include the categorisation of virgin olive oils according to their organoleptic characteristics, which are defined by a panel of experts.

The method they use, known as the "organoleptic assessment of virgin olive oil", aims to establish the necessary criteria for assessing the different characteristics of the flavour of virgin olive oils and to develop the necessary principles of classification. The method employed is more or less as follows:

The panel of experts, who are able to identify the four main tastes (**sweet, salty, acid** and **bitter**), study the oils produced in the European Union countries and select a set of positive and negative attributes which are common to all oils. The positive attributes include fruitiness, sweet, bitter, spicy, leafy, grassy, etc. Negative aspects are those such as acid, mould, humidity, etc.

The tasters note down the intensity of the attribute or defect they have perceived in the oil. The panel chief assesses the data and finally classifies the quality of the oil being scrutinised.

The are three types of virgin olive oil:

· **Extra virgin olive oil**, which has impeccable aroma and taste, without defects of any kind. It should have an acidity of less than 1°.

· **Virgin olive oil**. Similar to extra virgin, though more understated, with possible defects that are undetectable by the consumer. Acidity should be below 2°.

· **Normal virgin olive oil**, which has good taste and acceptable aroma, with an acidity of around 3.3°.

Acidity has commonly been used to assess oils, though it can sometimes be misunderstood. Bearing in mind that biologically synthesised matter is neutral, the existence of free fatty acids is the result of an anomaly in the molecules. The acidity of an oil expresses the quantity of these free fatty acids. Many years' harvests have taught that oils with a very low degree of acidity may have defects which disqualify them as 'extra'. However, low acidity is a sign of quality.

Virgin olive oil is most appreciated for its nutritional value. Research and international conferences on the biological value of olive oil have proved the important role olive oil plays in our health.

Its composition of fatty acids is ideal for the human body, and large amounts of money are invested to research seed mutations with a similar composition to these acids.

Olive oil contains monounsaturated oleic acid, which increases the production of high density lipoproteins (HDL) that make cholesterol flow to the liver to be eliminated, rather than remaining as a deposit on the artery walls.

Olive oil also contains linoleic acid, which our body does not produce and which it takes from the vegetables we eat. Olive oil contains this particular fatty acid in a similar proportion to a mother's milk. Linoleic acid cannot be assimilated by our body without vitamin E, which is also present in olive oil.

Olive oil is the most digestible and the most easy to assimilate of all fats. It acts on the intestine to combat chronic constipation and is an essential nutrient for our cells.

The benefits of olive oil for bone development and the health of growing children are well-known. It is also important in old age.

These properties are ample justification for the consumption of a product such as olive oil, renowned the world over for its exceptional qualities.

Cristino Lobillo

The olive tree and its main by-product, olive oil, have been a constant element in the landscape, in the homes, in the customs and above all in the cuisine of the people who live by the shores of the Mediterranean, since time immemorial.

Preparation

Ajo blanco is a cold soup or gazpacho which is popular all over Spain. Start by crushing the almonds and garlic in a mortar or blender, until they form a smooth paste. Soak the bread in a little salted water and add to the paste, together with 4 tablespoons of oil, 6 of vinegar and a pinch of salt.

Slowly add water (around 1.5 litres), stirring constantly, until the mix reaches the desired consistency. Keep *ajo blanco* in the fridge until just before serving, and garnish with peeled, seedless grapes, croutons or pieces of peeled apple or pear.

AJO BLANCO
CHILLED GARLIC AND ALMOND SOUP

Ingredients (serves 4 or 5)

300 g shelled almonds
400 g breadcrumbs
6 tablespoons vinegar
4 cloves garlic
Olive oil
Salt

CREMA DE MEJILLONES
MUSSEL SOUP

Preparation

Put the mussels in a casserole with a little water and heat until they open. Remove and discard the shells and put the liquid from the pan to one side. Cut the mussels up into smallish pieces.

Chop the onion very finely and peel and chop the tomatoes. Melt the butter and olive oil and sauté the onion and tomato for a few minutes, then add the brandy and the stock from the mussels and allow to cook gently. Stir in the flour, then pour in the milk slowly. Add salt and cook for a few more minutes before removing from the heat. Blend the soup in a food processor. Sprinkle the chopped mussels on top and serve piping hot.

Ingredients (serves 4)

2 kg mussels
300 g tomatoes
2 glasses (200 ml) brandy
225 g flour
50 g butter

500 ml milk
1 small glass (100 ml) olive oil
1 onion
Salt

Preparation

Cook the crabs in a large pan with 750 ml of water and salt. When cooked, take out the crabs (keep the water), extract the flesh, chop into small pieces and put to one side.

Pour the crab water into a casserole and add the butter, olive oil, finely chopped onion and a touch of salt. Cook for half an hour, then pour in the brandy and heat until the alcohol evaporates.

Now add most of the crab meat, the cream and a touch of pepper and mix with the hand blender. Return to the heat for a few minutes, then purée the soup in a food processor until completely smooth. Sprinkle the remaining pieces of crab meat on top and serve.

CREMA DE NÉCORAS
CRAB SOUP

Ingredients (serves 4)

3 kg small crabs
100 g butter
1 l cream
1 glass (100 ml) brandy
2 medium-sized onions
White pepper
Half a glass (75 ml) olive oil
Salt

Preparation

Cook the unpeeled prawns in a pan with salted boiling water for 2 minutes. Allow to cool and strain the water through a sieve. Mix the flour, vinegar and a little of the prawn water (which must be cold) in a shallow bowl and stir with a fork to form a smooth paste.

Whisk the egg white until stiff and carefully fold into the mixture. Peel the prawns, discard the heads, and roll them in the batter mixture one by one. Fry them straight away in plenty of hot oil.

When they are golden brown, remove from the pan and place them on kitchen paper for a moment before serving them piping hot.

GAMBAS REBOZADAS
PRAWNS IN BATTER

Ingredients (serves 4)

250 g prawns
150 g flour
1 egg white
1 tablespoon vinegar
Olive oil
Salt

Preparation

The home of gazpacho is without doubt Andalusia, though it is made throughout Spain. In the south, each household has its own gazpacho recipe, all slightly different but with the same basic principle and always delicious.

Wash the tomatoes and the green pepper, peel the cucumber and garlic, chop all four ingredients and place them in the blender together with a teaspoon of salt, the egg, the breadcrumbs, olive oil, a dash of vinegar and a glass of water.

Blend until smooth and pour into a bowl. Add around 1.5 litres of water and stir well. Check for salt and vinegar, adding more if necessary. Place the gazpacho in the fridge for a few minutes and serve well chilled.

GAZPACHO ANDALUZ
ANDALUSIAN GAZPACHO

Ingredients (serves 5 to 6)

1 green pepper
1 cucumber
1 kg tomatoes
1 clove garlic
1 egg
400 g breadcrumbs
Vinegar
1 small glass (150 ml) olive oil
Salt

Preparation

Clean the tuna, remove the skin and bones and cut into pieces. Place on a plate, season with salt and pour a dash of white wine over the top. Leave to marinate for a few minutes.

Prepare a stock with water, a bay leaf, a piece of onion, a dash of white wine and salt to taste. Bring to the boil, then simmer for a few minutes before adding the prawns. Bring back to the boil and cook for another 3 or 4 minutes, then remove the prawns from the stock and allow to cool before peeling them.

Chop the rest of the onion, heat a little olive oil in a frying pan and add the onion. When it begins to brown, add the tuna pieces and cook on a low heat for 10 to 15 minutes. Remove from the heat and blend in a food processor, together with the prawns, the fried tomato and the egg yolks.

Whisk the egg whites until stiff and fold them into the mixture, stirring carefully with a wooden spoon from bottom to top so as not to deflate the egg whites. Tip the mixture into an oven-proof dish greased with butter and cover with tin foil.

Place in the oven at a medium temperature for around an hour until the mixture has set, then remove and allow to cool. When it is completely cold, turn it out onto a platter and decorate with finely chopped lettuce around the edge. Serve with slices of toast and a light mayonnaise.

PATÉ DE BONITO
TUNA PÂTÉ

Ingredients (serves 4)

500 g tuna
500 g large prawns
4 tablespoons fried tomato
1 large onion
8 eggs, separated
White wine

1 bay leaf
Butter
Mayonnaise
Olive oil
Salt

Preparation

Heat a little olive oil in a casserole, chop the onion and fry until brown, then add 1 or 2 crushed garlic cloves, the ham, *tocino* and chorizo, all chopped into pieces, together with the beans (previously soaked for 12 hours). Now add 2.5 litres of water and season with salt and a touch of pepper. Cook for around 3 hours until the beans are soft.

When cooked, add a few croutons and serve.

SOPA ASTURIANA
ASTURIAN SOUP

Ingredients (serves 6)

250 g white beans	1 onion
100 g chorizo sausage	Bread (for croutons)
100 g salt pork (*tocino*)	Pepper
100 g ham	Olive oil
2 cloves garlic	Salt

Preparation

Bring 750 ml of water to the boil and add salt. Crush the garlic in a mortar with half a teaspoon of paprika and mix with a dash of olive oil. Add to the boiling water, together with the bread and the beaten egg. Stir well, cover and remove from the heat, leaving the soup to stand for 10 minutes before serving.

SOPA DE AJO
GARLIC SOUP

Ingredients (serves 2)

1 plate of leftover bread, in thin slices
1 clove garlic
1 egg
Olive oil
Paprika
Salt

SOPA DE PESCADO CON MAYONESA
FISH SOUP WITH MAYONNAISE

Preparation

Clean the fish and place in a pan with 1.5 to 2 litres of water, together with the chopped carrot, the garlic, a sprig of parsley, the chopped onion and salt. Cook for half an hour, then remove the fish and cut into small pieces. Place the pieces in a soup tureen and add the water, straining it through a sieve. With the soup still piping hot, dissolve 10 to 12 tablespoons of mayonnaise (preferably made with olive oil) into the soup, stirring carefully to make sure there are no lumps.

Serve immediately.

Ingredients (serves 5 or 6)

1 whiting	2 cloves garlic
1 head of hake	1 medium-sized onion
1 red mullet	Parsley
1 sole	Salt
2 carrots	Mayonnaise

Preparation

Wash the clams, changing the water frequently, and place them in a casserole with a small amount of water and white wine, the bay leaf and a sprig of thyme. Cook for five minutes, then remove and discard the shells.

In a second casserole, preferably earthenware, fry the chopped onion, crushed garlic and ham in olive oil. Stir well until the onion begins to brown, then add the clams together with their stock (previously strained), 1.5 litres of water, chopped parsley, salt and a few thinly sliced pieces of leftover bread. Cook for 2 or 3 minutes and serve.

This soup, together with the *zarauztarra* from Guipúzcoa, made with clams and liqueur, is popular throughout the north of Spain, particularly in the Basque country, from where it originates.

SOPA VASCA
BASQUE SOUP

Ingredients (serves 5 or 6)

Bread	3 cloves garlic
1 kg clams (or mussels)	Thyme
80 g diced ham	Olive oil
1 onion	Salt
White wine	
1 bay leaf	
Parsley	

Preparation

Cut the meat into even chunks, rub with garlic and put to one side for a few minutes, then add salt.

Brown the meat in a casserole with hot olive oil, then add the chopped onion and fry very gently. In a mortar, crush one clove of garlic and a sprig of parsley. Mix with a little white wine and pour over the meat.

Wash the artichokes and cook them for 15 minutes, then add them to the casserole to finish cooking.

When tender, place the meat and artichokes on a platter. Pour the sauce, which can be blended or left whole, over the top and decorate with strips of pepper.

ALCACHOFAS CON CARNE
ARTICHOKES WITH MEAT

Ingredients (serves 4)

12 artichokes	1 or 2 cloves garlic
500 g stewing meat	Parsley
1 fresh or tinned pepper	Olive oil
White wine	Salt
1 onion	

Preparation

Scorch the hen with alcohol to remove all the feather stubble, cut into small pieces, mix with crushed garlic and put to one side. After half an hour, season with salt and fry in hot oil. As the pieces brown, place them in a casserole. Crush a clove of garlic and a sprig of parsley in a mortar and mix with a dash of white wine. Chop the onion and fry in the same oil used for the hen. When it browns, add the tomato, the chopped peppers with their liquid and the garlic and parsley mixture. Fry for a few minutes, then add to the casserole and cook slowly until the hen is tender. Add a little cold water from time to time if necessary.

Having soaked the beans overnight, drain off the water and place the beans in a casserole with the onion, half a bay leaf, a sprig of parsley, a crushed garlic clove and olive oil. Cover with cold water, shake the pan and cook until tender, then season with salt and saffron, add breadcrumbs and cook on a low heat for 15 minutes until the stock thickens. Add the beans to the hen, shake the pan and cook on a low heat for another 30 minutes. Check for salt. Leave to stand for a few minutes before serving.

ALUBIAS CON GALLINA
KIDNEY BEANS WITH HEN

Ingredients (serves 4 or 6)

500 g hen	3 cloves garlic
500 g kidney beans	Parsley
1 onion	Saffron
1/2 tin tomatoes	Olive oil
1 small tin peppers	Salt
1/2 glass (75 ml) vinegar	

Preparation

Wash and peel the potatoes and cut them into thin slices, as if for a Spanish omelette. Once the cod is de-salted, cut into small strips. Peel and chop the tomatoes. Heat a little olive oil in a casserole and add the potatoes, cod and tomato. Stir well and add a tablespoon of paprika, cover the potatoes with boiling water and cook for half an hour.

In a mortar, crush the garlic, saffron and parsley and mix with a spoonful or two of the liquid from the casserole. Add salt and pour the mixture over the potatoes.

Make a dough with the flour and water and roll it out until it is very thin. Use a glass to cut out rounds and place them over the potatoes. Cook for a further 10 or 15 minutes and serve piping hot.

ANDRAJOS DE JAÉN
JAÉN TATTERS

Ingredients (serves 4)

500 g potatoes	Parsley
100 g cod	Saffron
200 g flour	Olive oil
250 g tomatoes	Salt
2 cloves garlic	Pepper
Paprika	

Preparation

Scrub the courgettes clean and remove the flesh from the inside using an apple corer or a spoon.

Finely chop an onion and fry in olive oil. When it is browned, add the mince, stir well and remove from the heat. Now chop the olives and two hard-boiled eggs and add them to the pan, together with the raisins. Use this mixture to stuff the courgettes and seal the end with a thin piece of onion peel. Beat the other egg, coat the courgettes in flour, dip them in the egg and fry in plenty of olive oil.

Once they are fried, place them in a casserole and cover them with the following sauce:

Finely chop an onion and fry in olive oil. When it begins to brown, add a tablespoon of flour, a dash of white wine and the stock (fresh or from a stock cube). Blend in a food processor, pour over the courgettes and cook until they are tender.

When they are cooked, remove them carefully from the casserole, making sure that they remain in one piece, and place them on a serving dish. Add the crushed almonds to the sauce and pour over the courgettes. If the sauce is too thick, add a little more stock.

CALABACINES RELLENOS
STUFFED COURGETTES

Ingredients (serves 4)

6 courgettes
3 eggs
100 g mince
2 onions
50 g stoned olives
50 g raisins (seedless)

2 tablespoons crushed almonds
White wine
Stock
Flour
Olive oil
Salt

Preparation

Brown the mince in a frying pan with olive oil, add the chopped garlic, 2 tablespoons of tomato sauce, one chopped pepper, a sprig of chopped parsley and a teaspoon of white wine. Cook for a few minutes and remove from the heat. Allow to cool before adding the egg, stirring the mixture well.

Prepare the onions by removing the tough layers of the peel, then use an apple corer or the point of a knife to extract the insides. Stuff them with the mixture and fry them in oil until they begin to brown. Remove the onions from the pan and place them in a casserole. Crush a clove of garlic and a sprig of parsley in a mortar with 100 ml of white wine, mix with the tomato sauce and pour over the onions. If the sauce needs thickening, stir in a tablespoon of flour.

Season with salt, a touch of chilli pepper and the bay leaf and cook the onions on a low heat until tender.

CEBOLLAS RELLENAS CON CARNE
STUFFED ONIONS

Ingredients (serves 6)

12 onions	2 cloves garlic
1 egg	Flour
250 g mince	1 red chilli pepper
Tomato sauce	1 bay leaf
1 small tin peppers	Parsley
White wine	Salt
Olive oil	

Preparation

Remove the leaves from the cauliflower and trim the stalk, leaving a solid stem. Cook the cauliflower in an uncovered saucepan in plenty of salted boiling water. When it is tender, remove from the pan taking care it does not break into pieces and place on a round ovenproof dish.

Cover with béchamel sauce and place the vegetables and chopped carrots round the edge. Place in the oven for a few minutes and serve.

The cauliflower can also be covered with mayonnaise and is often served on its own, with a simple olive oil and vinegar dressing.

COLIFLOR CON GUARNICIÓN
CAULIFLOWER WITH GARNISH

Ingredients (serves 6)

1 medium-sized cauliflower
1 small cabbage
1 tin peas
300 g carrots
Béchamel sauce
Salt

Preparation

If the tuna is fresh, season with salt and fry on a medium heat with olive oil until it is cooked on the inside and lightly browned on the outside. Remove from the pan, drain off any oil and cut into small pieces on a plate, removing the skin and any bones.

Heat 3 tablespoons of oil in a pan and fry the chopped onion and garlic and the peppers cut into thin strips. When all the ingredients are soft, add the tomato and a pinch of salt. Allow the sauce to thicken, then blend in a food processor. Add the tuna pieces and any juices given off, mix well and allow to cool. If the tuna is tinned, add directly to the sauce, draining the oil first.

On a floured surface, roll out half the pastry into a round, which should be 5 cm bigger than the mould to be used. Grease the mould with butter and sprinkle with a little flour, then roll the pastry onto a rolling pin and rest one edge on the side of the mould. Carefully unroll the pastry into the mould and when it is in place, prick with a fork.

Add the tuna and tomato sauce, cover with another layer of pastry using the same technique and seal the edges. Decorate the top of the *empanada* with overlaying strips of pastry to form a criss-cross or any other pattern of your choice. Brush the surface with egg to bring out a shine.

Place the pie in a pre-heated oven at 200° C until golden brown and cooked on the inside. Remove from the mould and serve either warm or cold.

EMPANADA DE BONITO
TUNA PASTRY PIE

Ingredients (serves 4)

600 g puff-pastry	1 medium-sized onion
500 g fresh or tinned tuna	1 clove garlic
250 g chopped tinned tomatoes	Olive oil
1 green pepper	Salt
1/2 red pepper	
1 egg	
Butter	
Flour	

Preparation

Wash the cauliflower carefully and cook in boiling salted water. When soft, remove from the pan, allow to cool and cut into bite-sized pieces, placing them in a salad bowl. Chop the ham or sausage, the olives and the parsley (optional) and add to the cauliflower.

Coat the salad with a light mayonnaise or a vinaigrette dressing and serve chilled.

ENSALADA DE COLIFLOR
CAULIFLOWER SALAD

Ingredients (serves 5 or 6)

1 cauliflower
Olives
1 slice ham or bologna sausage
Parsley
Mayonnaise

ESPÁRRAGOS VERDES CON YOGUR
GREEN ASPARAGUS WITH YOGHURT

Preparation

The asparagus should all be of equal thickness. Peel them from the tip down and cut to equal length (around 24 cm). Wash well and soak in cold water.

Bring a casserole with plenty of salted water to the boil and add the asparagus, making sure they are all facing the same way so as not to break the tips when removing them from the pan. Bring back to the boil and cook for 35 minutes.

When they are soft, drain well and cut into pieces 5 cm long (use only the tender part of the tips; the rest can be used for a soup or purée) and place on a serving dish covered with tin foil.

In a frying pan with olive oil, fry the breadcrumbs and curry powder, then add the juice of half a lemon and the two yoghurts. Stir well and cook for a few minutes on a low heat until the sauce is smooth and even.

Pour the sauce over the asparagus, place in the oven for a few minutes and serve hot.

Ingredients (serves 4)

1.5 kg thin green asparagus
2 cartons natural yoghurt
1/2 lemon
1 teaspoon curry powder
1 tablespoon breadcrumbs
Olive oil
Salt

Preparation

Wash the spinach well and cook in salted boiling water for 5 minutes, then soak the leaves in cold water, rinse well to remove all the water, chop them into strips and place in a casserole.

Chop the onion and two cloves of garlic and fry in olive oil. Add a teaspoon of paprika and a dash of vinegar and add the mixture to the spinach. Season with salt and cinnamon, cover and cook on a low heat for a few minutes.

Serve on a platter with slices of fried bread and the remaining cloves of garlic.

ESPINACAS AL ESTILO CORDOBÉS
CÓRDOBA-STYLE SPINACH

Ingredients (serves 6)

1 kg spinach
1 small onion
6 cloves garlic
Bread
Paprika
Vinegar
Cinnamon
Olive oil
Salt

Preparation

Leave the beans to soak in water for 12 hours, then place them in a casserole with around 8 tablespoons of olive oil, a chopped garlic clove, the chopped onion and the bay leaf. Cover with water, cover and bring to the boil. Simmer for an hour and a half to two hours (depending on the quality of the beans), stirring occasionally and adding cold water if necessary. When the beans are almost soft, add salt to taste.

In a second casserole, heat a little olive oil and add the other clove of garlic, finely chopped, making sure that it does not burn. Add the previously washed clams, the chopped parsley and the wine. Cover and cook until the clams open, then remove and discard one half of the shells. Add the prawns and cook for two or three minutes more. Pour this sauce over the beans and cook for five more minutes before serving.

FABAS CON ALMEJAS Y MARISCO
FABA BEANS WITH CLAMS AND SEAFOOD

Ingredients (serves 6)

750 g *fabas* (large white beans)	1 bay leaf
400 g clams	Chopped parsley
300 g large prawns (peeled)	Olive oil
1 small onion	Salt
1 glass (150 ml) white wine	
2 cloves garlic	

Preparation

Place the meat, the bone, the *tocino* and around 2 litres of water in a cooking pot. Bring to the boil, scooping off the froth which comes to the surface. When the water begins to boil, add the chickpeas (previously soaked), scooping off more froth if necessary. Add salt, the onion and parsley and cook on a low heat. Cook the chorizo separately.

When the chickpeas are soft, remove the stock with a ladle to make a soup, but leave some liquid to cook the potatoes, which should be cut into four if big or left whole if smaller. The potatoes should be cooked by the steam, making sure that they stay in one piece. For the soup, add pasta or bread, but only a small amount, as it should not be too thick. When the potatoes are cooked, drain off the remaining stock into the soup.

Serve the chickpeas on a platter with the potatoes, the meat and the chorizo cut into slices.

GARBANZOS EN PUCHERO
CHICKPEA HOTPOT

Ingredients (serves 6)

600 g chickpeas	1 piece onion
700 g potatoes	Parsley
500 g beef brisket	Saffron
100 g salt pork (*tocino*)	Salt
2 chorizo sausages	
1 bone	

Preparation

Finely chop the onion and fry in olive oil, together with the lettuce cut into julienne. Cut the ham into strips and add to the pan. Fry for a few minutes, then add the peas and stir well.

Cover the pan and cook on a moderate heat until the peas are soft, then add the cream, a tablespoon of chopped parsley, a pinch of nutmeg and another of pepper, check for salt and stir before removing from the heat. The peas can be served with slices of fried bread.

GUISANTES A LA CREMA CON JAMÓN
PEAS WITH CREAM AND HAM

Ingredients (serves 6)

500 g frozen peas	Pepper
50 g ham	Chopped parsley
1/2 onion	Nutmeg
1 lettuce	Salt
4 tablespoons cream	
1 small glass (100 ml) olive oil	

Preparation

Discard the outer leaves of the artichokes, wash and chop into four. Cut the *tocino* into small pieces, chop the lettuces and remove the green part of the spring onions.

Heat the olive oil in a casserole and add the *tocino*. Fry for a few minutes, then add the broad beans (the seeds should be removed), the lettuce hearts and the artichokes. Sprinkle with salt and continue frying for a few more minutes. Cover the casserole and remove from the heat for 15 minutes, shaking the pan from time to time, without removing the lid. Then add the flour, stock, parsley and pepper and simmer for 40 minutes until the beans are tender.

HABAS A LA HORTELANA
BROAD BEANS WITH VEGETABLES

Ingredients (serves 6)

1 kg broad beans
4 artichokes
2 lettuce hearts
6 spring onions
125 g salt pork (*tocino*)
1 small glass (100 ml) olive oil

250 ml stock
1 tablespoon flour
Parsley
Pepper
Salt

Preparation

Top and tail the beans if they are thin and not too stringy. If they are hard, cut away the top layer with a knife. In either case, wash them well and cook in salted boiling water, adding a clove of garlic, the onion and the parsley. Drain off the water once they are cooked and put the garlic, parsley and onion to one side.

Separately, fry the other clove of garlic in olive oil. When it browns, remove and pour the oil over the beans, adding a dash of vinegar. Serve in an oval dish, decorated with chopped hard-boiled egg.

JUDÍAS VERDES CON HUEVO
GREEN BEANS WITH EGG

Ingredients (serves 6)

1.5 kg green beans
2 hard-boiled eggs
1/2 onion
2 cloves garlic
1 sprig parsley
Vinegar
Olive oil
Salt

Preparation

Wash the beans and remove the side threads. Chop into 3-4 cm-long pieces. Place them in a pan and cover with salted water and a tablespoon of lemon juice. Cover the pan and cook for 25 to 30 minutes until tender.

Heat a generous amount of olive oil in a casserole and gently fry the onion, chopped into rings, until it becomes transparent. Cut the ham into small pieces and add to the onion, stir well and add the flour. Stir the flour in well, then slowly pour in around 100 ml of the water used to cook the beans, making sure that no lumps of flour are formed. Dissolve a tablespoon of mustard in the juice of the lemon and add to the casserole together with the beans. Stir well, bring to the boil, check for salt and serve.

JUDÍAS VERDES CON MOSTAZA
GREEN BEANS WITH MUSTARD

Ingredients (serves 6)

1 kg green beans
1 large onion
100 g cured ham (*jamón serrano*)
2 tablespoons flour
1 lemon
Olive oil
Salt

Preparation

Wash the cabbage leaves well and cook them in salted boiling water for 5 minutes. Drain and leave them to cool.

Heat a little olive oil in a frying pan and brown the mince, adding a pinch of nutmeg and another of salt. Remove the mince onto a plate, chop the *tocino* and ham and add to the pan together with a few stoned black olives. When browned, mix everything together and spread onto the cabbage leaves, making rolls. Close them up with toothpicks or by tying them to make sure none of the filling comes out. Coat them in egg and breadcrumbs and fry them in plenty of olive oil.

When they are fried, remove the thread or twine (the toothpicks can be left in place) and serve.

LIADILLOS SEVILLANOS
SEVILLIAN CABBAGE ROLLS

Ingredients (serves 6)

12 white cabbage leaves	Nutmeg
100 g mince	Black olives
50 g salt pork (*tocino*)	Breadcrumbs
50 g ham	Olive oil
1 egg	Salt

Preparation

Soak the lentils for two hours. Chop one of the onions, the garlic, pepper and tomato and place them in a casserole together with the lentils. Add the bay leaf, the paprika and almost all the olive oil. Cover with water, put the lid on the pot and simmer gently for an hour or more until the lentils are tender. Add salt before removing from the heat.

Heat the remaining olive oil in a frying pan, chop the second onion and fry gently until browned, then add the sliced bacon and fry for two or three more minutes. Add to the lentils, check for salt, add a dash of raw olive oil, cover and cook for five more minutes. Serve piping hot.

LENTEJAS GUISADAS
STEWED LENTILS

Ingredients (serves 6)

500 g lentils
2 medium-sized onions
2 cloves garlic
1 bay leaf
1 green pepper

1 tomato
1 rasher bacon
1 teaspoon paprika
1 small glass (100 ml) olive oil
Salt

Preparation

Place the beans in a casserole and cover with cold water, without salt. Bring to the boil, then drain off the water and add cold water again, with 100 ml of olive oil, half an onion cut into pieces, the bay leaf and cloveof garlic and cook on a low heat for 2 or 3 hours (depending on the beans). Stir the pan from time to time, adding more cold water if necessary. Add salt towards the end of the cooking time, when there should be little liquid left.

When the beans are tender, turn them out onto a platter and decorate with small mounds of boiled white rice, shaped with a small cup or similar recipient. Hard-boiled eggs and chopped parsley can also be sprinkled over the top.

This is a very traditional Spanish dish, particularly in the southern part of the Levant region, where the annual festival of Moors and Christians is celebrated.

MOROS Y CRISTIANOS
MOORS AND CHRISTIANS (BLACK BEANS WITH WHITE RICE)

Ingredients (serves 6)

400 g black beans
250 g rice
1 onion
1 clove garlic
1 bay leaf
Olive oil
Salt

Preparation

Finely chop the onion and fry in olive oil. When it begins to brown, add the vegetables. Stir well, cover and cook for 10 minutes. Mix the stock with a dash of sherry or brandy and add to the vegetables. Add the stock (either fresh or from a stock cube) and cook for a few more minutes without the lid, until the alcohol has evaporated.

Cover the pan again and cook on a low heat until the vegetables are soft, then beat the eggs and add them to the pan, together with the prawns. Stir well, bring back to the boil and simmer for a further 5 minutes, stirring occasionally so that the egg cooks but does not stick. Check for salt and serve.

PANACHÉ DE VERDURAS
MIXED VEGETABLES

Ingredients (serves 6)

1 kg assorted frozen vegetables
150 g peeled prawns
3 eggs
1 onion
1 cup (250 ml) stock
Dry sherry or brandy
Olive oil
Salt

Preparation

Soak the cod overnight to remove the salt, changing the water at least twice. Crush the garlic, cut the pepper into squares, peel and chop the potatoes and the tomato and cut the cod into pieces. Heat the olive oil in a frying pan and add the garlic. When it begins to brown, add the other ingredients, together with a teaspoon of paprika.

Stir well and cook for a few minutes, then cover with warm water and cook on a low heat for half an hour. Shake the pan a few times to make sure that nothing sticks to the bottom.

When everything is cooked, check for salt and leave to stand for 5 minutes before serving. Cayenne pepper can also be added for a spicy touch.

PATATAS CON BACALAO Y PIMIENTO
POTATOES WITH COD AND PEPPER

Ingredients (serves 4)

1 kg potatoes
3 thin pieces of cod
1 green pepper
1 soft tomato
2 cloves garlic
4 or 5 tablespoons olive oil
Paprika
Salt

Preparation

Heat a few tablespoons of olive oil in a casserole, add the garlic cloves and fry until brown, then remove and put to one side. Chop the onion into thin rings and add to the casserole. Cover and allow them to fry gently. Remove the skin and bones from the tuna and cut into pieces. Peel and chop the potatoes and add both ingredients to the casserole. Cover with hot water and add the bay leaf.

In a mortar, crush the garlic, chopped parsley, the chilli pepper and the peeled and chopped tomato. Add a dash of white wine, mix well and add to the casserole. Season with salt and cook until the potatoes are soft. Place a few slices of toasted bread on top and place in the oven for five minutes, then leave to stand for a further five minutes and serve in the same casserole.

This is a traditional sailors' dish from the Cantabrian area. In the Basque Country it is known as *marmitako* and in Santander as *marmita*.

PATATAS CON BONITO (MARMITAKO)
TUNA AND POTATO CASSEROLE

Ingredients (serves 6)

1 kg potatoes	Parsley
500 g tuna	1 red chilli pepper
2 onions	Bread
1 tomato	1 bay leaf
2 cloves garlic	Olive oil
1 small glass (100 ml) white wine	Salt

Preparation

Peel and wash the potatoes and boil for 10 to 12 minutes. Meanwhile, separate the cauliflower into pieces, peel the onion and slice into rings. When the potatoes are cooked, drain and allow to cool.

Heat a tablespoon of oil in a pan and add the mustard powder. Stir until it is toasted, then add freshly ground pepper and the onion. Stir well and add the crushed garlic and the cauliflower and fry for around 5 minutes, then add half a litre of salted water.

Chop the potatoes and add them to the cauliflower. Cook for 10 minutes, then add the chopped tomato and the juice of one lemon. Cook for a few minutes more on a moderate heat until the sauce thickens slightly and serve.

PATATAS CON COLIFLOR
POTATOES WITH CAULIFLOWER

Ingredients (serves 4)

500 g potatoes
1 large cauliflower
1 onion
1 clove garlic
1 tomato

1 lemon
Mustard powder
Pepper
Olive oil
Salt

PATATAS GUISADAS CON VERDURA
STEWED POTATOES WITH VEGETABLES

Preparation

Chop the chorizo sausage into pieces and the ham into small squares and fry both in a casserole with olive oil. Finely chop the onion, add to the pan and, when browned, stir in the crushed garlic and parsley. Stir well and add the potatoes, peeled and left whole (use small, evenly sized potatoes), half a tablespoon of flour, the lettuce hearts and a little stock or water. Cook for a few minutes and then add the peas. Continue cooking until the sauce thickens. Before serving, check for salt and sprinkle finely chopped parsley over the top.

Ingredients (serves 4)

500 g potatoes	2 cloves garlic
200 g peas	Chopped parsley
3 lettuce hearts	Flour
1/2 chorizo sausage	Olive oil
100 g ham	Salt
1/2 onion	

Preparation

Crush a clove of garlic and a sprig of parsley in a mortar, mix in with the mince and leave to stand for 15 minutes. Then season with salt and brown the mince in a frying pan with a little olive oil. Cook the potatoes whole in salted boiling water, then rinse them in cold water and put to one side.

Make a thick béchamel sauce with milk, flour and butter, adding a little grated onion half way during the process. Then add the mince, stir a few times to mix it all together and allow to cool.

Heat a little olive oil in a frying pan and brown the onion. Add the chopped tomatoes and cook until the sauce thickens, then add a crushed clove of garlic and a dash of white wine. Cook for a few more minutes, then blend the sauce in a food processor and pour into an ovenproof dish.

When the potatoes have cooled, peel them and cut off one end. Hollow them out and fill them with the mince mixture. Place them on top of the sauce, making sure there is enough room for the potatoes to sit without touching each other.

Chop the cabbage leaves and the carrots and cook in salted boiling water, then drain. Chop the ham into squares and fry in a little olive oil. Add the vegetables, stir well and cook for 10 minutes. Now add the chopped pepper with any juices from the tin (if fresh, chop and fry first), stir well and place around the potatoes. Add a knob of butter to each potato and place in a hot oven for 10 minutes. When cooked, decorate each potato with a strip of pepper and serve in the same dish.

PATATAS REALES CON GUARNICIÓN
ROYAL POTATOES WITH GARNISH

Ingredients (serves 6)

1 kg evenly sized potatoes	2 cloves garlic
50 g ham	White wine
500 g mince	Butter
250 ml milk	1 tablespoon flour
1 kg tomatoes	Parsley
1 fresh or tinned pepper	Olive oil
150 g carrots	Salt
1 onion	
Cabbage leaves	

Preparation

Clean the peppers, cut away the stem and discard the seeds. Put the stem to one side to use later. Season the mince with salt and pepper to taste, the chopped garlic and a sprig of parsley.

Heat a few tablespoons of olive oil in a frying pan and brown the mince. Chop the onion, add to the pan and cook on a low heat for 10 minutes. If the mince becomes too dry, add a little stock or water.

Stir in the fried tomato and continue cooking for a few minutes before beating the egg and adding it to the pan, together with the rice and salt to taste. Stir well to mix all the ingredients together and use the mixture to stuff the peppers.

Place the stems back on the peppers and put them in an earthenware casserole or ovenproof dish. Dribble with olive oil and place in the oven at a moderate to high temperature for around 35 minutes until they are tender.

While they are cooking, baste them in the juices they give off and turn them over carefully if necessary. When they are ready, remove them from the oven and leave them to stand for 5 minutes covered with a clean tea towel. Peel off the skin, sprinkle with chopped parsley and serve.

PIMIENTOS RELLENOS DE CARNE
PEPPERS STUFFED WITH MINCE

Ingredients (serves 4)

8 fresh red peppers	2 cloves garlic
500 g mince	1 egg
50 g boiled rice	Olive oil
100 g onion	Parsley
2 glasses (300 ml) fried tomato (fresh or tinned)	Pepper
	Salt

Preparation

Prepare a thick béchamel sauce with the milk, butter and flour, then add the desalted cod, cut into small pieces. Cook for a few minutes until the sauce is quite thick, then add a beaten egg and stir well. With this mixture prepared, wash the peppers and cut away the tops with a knife, taking care to keep them whole (remove the seeds). Fill the peppers with the mixture and close them up by putting the tops back on. Coat them in flour, dip them in egg and fry in hot olive oil. When they are browned, place them loosely in a casserole.

Prepare a sauce by chopping the onion and frying in olive oil together with the peeled carrot, the tomato, a clove of garlic and a chopped sprig of parsley, with a dash of white wine. Season with salt and cook on a high heat until all the ingredients are soft. Blend in a food processor and pour over the peppers.

Now cook the peppers gently on a low heat, shaking the casserole from time to time so that they do not stick and placing a fish slice under them so they remain loose. Serve on a platter with the sauce over the top.

PIMIENTOS RELLENOS DE BACALAO
PEPPERS STUFFED WITH COD

Ingredients (serves 4)

Peppers for stuffing	Flour
200 g cod	White wine
2 eggs	1 onion
250 g tomatoes	1 clove garlic
1 carrot	Parsley
Butter	Olive oil
Milk	Salt

Preparation

Chop the onions and fry them gently (without browning them) in a large frying pan. Roast the peppers slightly to remove the skin, chop into pieces and remove the seeds. Peel and chop the courgette. Wash and peel the tomatoes and chop into small pieces, removing the seeds. Add the peppers, courgette and tomatoes to the pan and continue frying. Add salt. Finally, when everything is cooked, beat the eggs and add them to the pan, stirring until they set. Serve hot in an earthenware casserole or similar recipient.

PISTO
RATATOUILLE

Ingredients (serves 4)

3 eggs
500 g onions
500 g tomatoes
1 courgette
3 peppers
Olive oil
Salt

Preparation

Wash the tomatoes and hollow them out, keeping the flesh. Season with salt and put them to one side.

Prepare a béchamel sauce by melting half the butter in a saucepan and when it starts to brown, add the flour, stir well and pour in the milk, previously brought to the boil. Season with salt and cook for 10 minutes. Chop the eggs into small pieces and add to the sauce. Pour it into a bowl and allow to cool.

Heat 3 tablespoons of olive oil in a frying pan and when it is hot, fry the onion without letting it brown too much, then add the chopped tomato and allow to cook for a few minutes. Crush the clove of garlic in a mortar, add a dash of white wine and add to the sauce. Cook until it reduces, check for salt and blend in a food processor. Keep the sauce warm.

Stuff the tomatoes with the cold béchamel sauce and place them in an ovenproof dish. Melt the rest of the butter and pour over the tomatoes. Sprinkle the grated cheese and a pinch of salt over the top and place in the oven at a high temperature for 15 minutes.

Serve with the sauce spooned around the tomatoes.

TOMATES RELLENOS
STUFFED TOMATOES

Ingredients (serves 6)

12 medium-sized tomatoes	White wine
2 hard-boiled eggs	1 tablespoon flour
50 g grated cheese	50 g butter
500 g tomatoes for sauce	1 clove garlic
2 tablespoons chopped onion	Olive oil
500 ml milk	Salt

Preparation

Put the cod to soak for 24 hours before using, changing the water twice during this time. Peel the potatoes and place in a pan together with the desalted cod and cover with plenty of cold water. Bring to the boil then reduce the heat to the minimum and simmer slowly for 25 minutes.

When the cod is cooked, remove the skin and bones and flake into pieces. Mash the potatoes and mix with the cod, adding a finely chopped clove of garlic and chopped parsley. Separate the eggs and add the yolks one by one to the fish and potato. Whisk the egg whites until stiff and fold into the mixture, stirring well.

Heat plenty of olive oil in a frying pan and form the fritters by scooping out a small ball of the mixture with a spoon. When the oil is hot, fry the fritters 5 or 6 at a time until golden brown. Remove from the oil and place them on kitchen paper to absorb any excess oil. Serve hot.

BUÑUELOS DE BACALAO
COD FRITTERS

Ingredients (serves 6)

700 g dried salt cod
1.5 kg potatoes
3 eggs
1 clove garlic
1 tablespoon chopped parsley
Olive oil

Preparation

Wipe the mushrooms clean and separate the heads from the stems. Pour lemon juice over the heads to stop them turning brown. Remove some of the flesh from the heads and put to one side.

Heat a little olive oil in a casserole and fry 2 cloves of garlic, one onion and parsley, all finely chopped. When the onions begin to brown, add the chopped mushroom stems and one glass of dry sherry. While this is cooking, beat the eggs, season with salt and pepper and scramble them in a frying pan with a little olive oil. The eggs should still be quite runny. When the mushrooms are cooked, add to the eggs and check for salt. Use this mixture to stuff the heads of the mushrooms and place them on a greased ovenproof dish.

In a separate pan, prepare a sauce by frying the other onion, 2 cloves of garlic and the green pepper, all finely chopped, the mushroom pieces extracted from the heads and the flour. Mix well and pour in the second glass of wine and a little water. Cook on a medium heat until the pepper is soft, then blend the mixture in a food processor. Check for salt and sprinkle in a sprig of chopped parsley. Pour the sauce over the stuffed mushroom heads.

Finally, place the dish in a pre-heated oven at a high temperature for 10 minutes. Serve while the mushrooms are still piping hot.

CHAMPIÑONES RELLENOS
STUFFED MUSHROOMS

Ingredients (serves 4)

1 kg large mushrooms	2 large onions
1 green pepper	4 cloves garlic
4 eggs	Parsley
1 lemon	Pepper
2 glasses (200 ml) dry sherry	Olive oil
1 teaspoon flour	Salt

Preparation

Boil the green beans in salted water, then drain and put to one side. Peel and dice the potatoes and fry in olive oil. Chop the onion and half of the ham and fry until the onion softens, then add the chopped tomato, stirring well. Slice the green beans and add together with the peas, the potatoes and the red pepper, chopped into small pieces. Add salt.

Spoon this mixture onto six oven-proof plates or small dishes. Crack an egg onto each of the plates on top of the mixture and place in a pre-heated oven at a high temperature until the eggs set. Remove from the oven and garnish with the fried chorizo and the rest of the ham, both chopped into small pieces, together with the asparagus tips and a few strips of red pepper. Flamenco eggs should be served straight from the oven.

HUEVOS A LA FLAMENCA
FLAMENCO EGGS

Ingredients (serves 6)

6 eggs
1 tin of peas
100 g green beans
100 g potatoes
1 cup (250 ml) chopped tomatoes
100 g cured ham (*jamón serrano*)

100 g chorizo sausage
1 small tin red peppers
1 small tin asparagus tips
1 onion
Olive oil
Salt

Preparation

Wash the lettuce leaves, chop into small pieces and place in the middle of a round dish. Slice the tomatoes (which should not be too soft) in half, remove the seeds and place face up on the dish around the lettuce. Inside each tomato, place half a hard-boiled egg with the yolk face up and sprinkle with the grated carrot and finely chopped black olives.

Slice the pepper into strips and place in the middle of the dish, on top of the lettuce, in the shape of a star. Place the artichokes in between the tomatoes, alternating one of each, and place a small amount of mayonnaise on top of each artichoke. Finally, roll up the anchovies and dot them around the dish. Prepare a dressing of olive oil, lemon juice and salt and add just before serving.

HUEVOS A LA JARDINERA
EGGS WITH GARDEN VEGETABLES

Ingredients (serves 4)

4 hard-boiled eggs
2 tinned red peppers
2 carrots, grated
4 small tomatoes
1 lettuce
100 g stoned black olives
1 small tin artichokes
2 tins rolled anchovy fillets

250 ml mayonnaise
1 lemon
1/2 glass (100 ml) olive oil
Salt

Preparation

The first thing to do is to blend the peas in a food processor. If fresh, they should be cooked in salted boiling water for 15 minutes and allowed to cool before being blended. Now fry 2 cloves of garlic in olive oil, adding a small amount of water and a pinch of salt once browned. Allow to cook for a few minutes until the sauce thickens slightly, then add to the peas.

Season the mince with garlic, parsley and salt. Brown in a frying pan with a little olive oil, add the chopped ham, then turn the heat down. Chop the green beans into small pieces and boil in salted water together with the peeled and diced carrots. When cooked, drain and coat with a little olive oil.

Turn the mashed peas out onto a dish. Slice the eggs lengthways and remove the yolks, which should be added to the mince. Use this mixture to stuff the egg whites, then place them face down on the peas. Garnish with the green beans and carrots. If there is any leftover mince, place on top of the peas and serve.

HUEVOS COSTA VERDE
COSTA VERDE EGGS

Ingredients (serves 6)

6 hard-boiled eggs
1 large tin peas (or equivalent fresh peas)
500 g green beans
250 g carrots
50 g cooked ham

100 g mince
3 cloves garlic
Parsley
Olive oil
Salt

Preparation

Boil the potatoes without peeling them in salted water. When they are half-cooked, remove from the heat, peel and cut into slices. Coat them in flour and one of the eggs (beaten), fry with plenty of oil and put to one side.

In a second frying pan, heat a little olive oil and brown the mince, ham and chopped carrot, then add the tomato, the sherry and a little water. Simmer for 15 minutes, then season with salt and pepper.

Bring a saucepan of water with 2 tablespoons of vinegar to the boil and poach the 6 remaining eggs. Place on a dish or round plate with the potatoes round the edge and cover with the hot tomato and mince sauce. Serve immediately.

This dish from the Canary Isles can also be served with boiled rice and covered with a pepper or curry sauce.

HUEVOS AL ESTILO CANARIO
CANARY ISLES-STYLE EGGS

Ingredients (serves 6)

7 eggs	1 glass (100 ml) dry sherry
150 g mince	Flour
100 g ham	Vinegar
500 g potatoes	Pepper
1 large carrot	Olive oil
2 chopped tomatoes	Salt

Preparation

Wash and slice the mushrooms and put to one side. Wash and chop the chard and scald in boiling salted water for 2 or 3 minutes, then drain in a colander. Chop and fry one of the onions until it begins to brown, then add the mushrooms and the chard, season with salt and pepper and cook on a low heat for a few minutes, stirring regularly.

Beat the eggs with the cream, then add the mushrooms and chard to this mixture. Grease a pie mould and pour the mixture in. Bake at a medium temperature in a bain-marie until it sets and remove from the oven. Allow to cool and remove from the mould.

While the pie is baking, prepare the sauce. Finely chop the other onion, chop the leek into thin slices and grate the carrot. Melt a knob of butter in a saucepan and fry the onion, leek and carrot, together with the wine and a little water. Cook on a low heat until the vegetables are soft, add salt to taste and blend in a food processor. Serve the pie with the sauce on top.

PASTEL DE SETAS
WILD MUSHROOM PIE

Ingredients (serves 4)

400 g wild mushrooms	Knob of butter
100 g chard (*acelgas*)	1 glass (100 ml) sherry
1 carrot	2 onions
1 leek	Pepper
4 eggs	Olive oil
1 small glass (100 ml) cream	Salt

Preparation

Peel and wash the potatoes, cut into thin pieces and season with salt. Heat a generous amount of oil in a frying pan and fry the potatoes slowly, turning them 2 or 3 times. Drain the oil and make two identical potato omelettes, using 2 eggs for each. They should be ever so slightly underdone, with the insides still juicy.

Chop the onion finely and fry very gently in olive oil. When the onion begins to brown, add the tuna and stir together for a few minutes, before turning onto a plate, draining off any excess oil. With the two remaining eggs, make another omelette with the onion and tuna, the same size as the other two.

Fry the tomato in a little olive oil until it thickens, then blend in a food processor and season with salt.

Take a round dish and place first the tomato sauce, then one of the potato omelettes followed by a layer of béchamel sauce, making sure to cover all the surface of the omelette. Place the onion and tuna omelette on top and cover with another layer of béchamel. Finally, place the second potato omelette on top and cover with mayonnaise. Drain the peas, coat in a little olive oil and use them together with strips of pepper to decorate the edges of the 'cake'. As an alternative, hard-boiled egg and pieces of cured or cooked ham can also be used as decoration.

PASTEL DE TORTILLAS
OMELETTE CAKE

Ingredients (serves 4)

6 eggs
500 g potatoes
1 tin peppers
1 small tin peas
1 small tin chopped tomatoes
Mayonnaise

1 large cup (250 ml) béchamel sauce
1 large onion
Olive oil
Salt

Preparation

Wash the unpeeled potatoes and boil in salted water until soft, then drain and allow to cool before peeling them. Slice them lengthways and scoop out some of the flesh (put to one side) to create a hollow for the stuffing.

Wash the mushrooms carefully and chop into small pieces. Melt a knob of butter in a casserole with a little olive oil and fry the chopped onion and garlic until brown, then add the mushrooms, the juice of the lemon, the flour and the wine or brandy. Heat until the liquid evaporates and add the milk, stirring constantly, and the cream. Season with salt and pepper and add the scooped-out flesh from the potatoes. Sprinkle with parsley and cook until the mushrooms are soft.

Fill the hollowed-out potatoes with the stuffing and place in a greased ovenproof dish. Spread any remaining mixture over the potatoes. Heat in the oven for 5 minutes and serve hot.

RELLENO DE SETAS
WILD MUSHROOM STUFFING

Ingredients (serves 6)

750 g wild mushrooms	1 lemon
6 large potatoes	2 onions
1 tablespoon flour	1 clove garlic
1 glass (200 ml) milk	Parsley
1 glass (200 ml) cream	Pepper
Knob of butter	Olive oil
1 glass (100 ml) sherry or brandy	Salt

Preparation

Peel and wash the potatoes, cut into thin slices and season with salt (finely chopped onion or garlic is also added in many parts of Spain). Heat plenty of oil in a frying pan and fry the potatoes slowly, turning them 2 or 3 times. When soft, but before they begin to crisp, remove from the heat and place the potatoes in a colander to drain off the oil.

Beat the eggs well in a large bowl, season with salt and add the potatoes, mixing well so that the egg covers all the potatoes. Heat a little olive oil in a medium-sized frying pan and pour in the egg and potato, shaking the pan vigorously so that the mixture does not stick. Brown one side of the omelette then turn it over using a plate or saucepan lid and cook the other side. Spanish omelette is delicious served either hot or cold.

The omelette can also be made with onion. This should be finely chopped and fried along with the potatoes.

TORTILLA ESPAÑOLA
SPANISH OMELETTE

Ingredients (serves 6)

6 eggs
750 g potatoes
Olive oil
Salt

Preparation

Chop the rabbit into pieces, sprinkle with salt and place in a casserole with olive oil, the crushed garlic, a pinch of pepper and a small glass (100 ml) of water. Cook until the meat is tender, adding small amounts of water if it dries out.

Peel the tomatoes and remove the seeds. Fry them in olive oil with the chopped peppers, then add to the rabbit with a sprig of chopped parsley. Add the rice, stir well and pour in a litre of boiling water. Check for salt and simmer for 20 minutes. After this time, remove from the heat and leave to stand for 5 more minutes before serving.

ARROZ CON CONEJO
RICE WITH RABBIT

Ingredients (serves 4)

400 g rice
1 small rabbit
2 peppers
4 tomatoes
2 cloves garlic
Parsley
Pepper
Olive oil
Salt

Preparation

Chop the onion into small pieces and fry in a casserole with the butter and olive oil. When it begins to brown, add the rice, a sprig of chopped parsley and a teaspoon of paprika (or cayenne pepper) and stir well with a wooden spoon for a few minutes.

Bring the stock to the boil and add to the pan, season with salt and pepper and bring back to the boil. Shake the casserole a few times and add the raw peeled prawns, the peas and asparagus. Stir well and cook on a moderate heat for 20 minutes.

Remove from the heat and leave to stand for 10 minutes before serving.

ARROZ CON GAMBAS Y VERDURAS
RICE WITH PRAWNS AND VEGETABLES

Ingredients (serves 4)

1.5 cups (300 g) long grain rice	Parsley
500 g peeled prawns	Pepper
1 small onion	Paprika
1 small tin peas	Olive oil
1 small tin asparagus	Salt
1 l stock (fresh or stock cubes)	
45 g butter	

Preparation

Heat 5 tablespoons of olive oil in a large casserole. Chop the onion into small pieces and fry until it begins to brown, then add the meat, previously seasoned with salt and pepper and stir with a wooden spoon for a few minutes so that it does not become lumpy.

Add the fried tomato, mix in well and add the rice, the wine and the stock, stirring constantly. Check for salt and simmer for 20 minutes.

After this time remove the casserole from the heat, cover and leave to stand for at least 5 minutes before serving.

ARROZ RIOJANO
LA RIOJA RICE

Ingredients (serves 4)

1 large cup (250 g) rice
250 g mince
1 onion
1 cup (250 ml) red Rioja wine
1 tablespoon fried tomato
1 cup (250 ml) stock (fresh or stock cubes)
Pepper
Olive oil
Salt

ESPAGUETIS CON MARISCO
SEAFOOD SPAGHETTI

Preparation

Cook the prawns in salted boiling water for 2 or 3 minutes in order to peel them. Wash the mussels and clams thoroughly, changing the water frequently, and place them in a casserole with a dash of white wine, water and olive oil and cook for a few minutes until the shells open. Remove and discard the shells and place the stock to one side.

Heat a little olive oil in a second casserole and sauté the cloves of garlic (left whole). Then remove and discard the garlic and add the peeled prawns, clams, mussels, and the peeled and chopped tomatoes, together with the stock, which should be strained through a very fine sieve or muslin. Season with salt and cook for around 15 minutes until the tomatoes are soft, then add the chopped parsley.

Cook the spaghetti in salted boiling water for around 10 minutes. Drain and place in a large bowl and stir in the sauce. Serve hot.

Ingredients (serves 6)

500 g spaghetti	White wine
400 g clams	2 cloves garlic
250 g prawns	Parsley
1 kg mussels	Olive oil
500 g tomatoes	Salt

Preparation

Cut the pork into cubes, season with salt and pepper and put to one side. Chop the garlic and a sprig of parsley and fry in a casserole with a little olive oil. When the garlic begins to brown, add the meat and stir well to coat it in oil before adding the tomato sauce.

Stir well and simmer for 10 minutes on a low heat, then add the noodles, the paprika or cayenne and the stock, which should be brought to the boil first. Stir well to mix all the ingredients together and cook for a further 10 minutes.

When the noodles are cooked, check for salt and serve with grated cheese sprinkled on top.

FIDEOS A LA CAZUELA
NOODLE CASSEROLE

Ingredients (serves 4)

250 g short noodles (*fideos*), medium thickness
200 g pork
1 l stock (fresh or stock cubes)
2 cloves garlic
5 tablespoons tomato sauce
1 teaspoon paprika/cayenne pepper

3 tablespoons grated cheese
Olive oil
Parsley
Salt

Preparation

Cook the noodles in plenty of salted boiling water for 10 minutes, then drain.

While the pasta is cooking, cut the garlic into very thin slices and fry in olive oil until they begin to turn golden brown. Now add the finely chopped herbs -mint, basil, rosemary and a touch of parsley- and allow to cook slowly for a few minutes.

When the pasta is cooked, place in a large bowl and add the herbs, stirring well so it all mixes together. Serve quickly before the pasta cools down.

FIDEOS A LAS FINAS HIERBAS
NOODLES WITH HERBS

Ingredients (serves 4)

500 g noodles (*fideos*)
2 cloves garlic
75 g fresh mint
75 g basil
50 g rosemary
Parsley
Olive oil
Salt

Preparation

Finely chop the onion and fry in a little olive oil until it begins to brown. Add the peeled and chopped tomatoes, half a tablespoon of sugar to remove the acidity of the tomatoes and season to taste. Leave to cook slowly for a few minutes.

Meanwhile, crush a clove of garlic and a sprig of parsley in a mortar, add a few drops of vinegar and add to the tomato sauce and the clams. Add water if the sauce becomes too thick.

When the clams begin to open, which should take no more than 2 or 3 minutes, remove from the heat. Discard the shells and put the clams to one side. When the sauce is ready, blend in a food processor and leave to stand in a warm place.

Cook the pasta in plenty of salted boiling water for 10 minutes. Drain the pasta and mix with the sauce and clams. Serve hot in a large dish with a sprinkle of white pepper on top.

MACARRONES CON ALMEJAS
MACARONI WITH CLAMS

Ingredients (serves 4)

400 g macaroni	Parsley
500 g clams	White pepper
3 tomatoes	Sugar
1 onion	Olive oil
White wine	Salt
Garlic	

MACARRONES CON CHIPIRONES
MACARONI WITH CUTTLEFISH

Preparation

Finely chop the onion and garlic and fry in hot olive oil. When they begin to brown, add the cuttlefish, stir well and cook for a few minutes. Add a dash of dry white wine and simmer on a low heat for 5 minutes.

Add the fried tomato, stir well and continue cooking until the cuttlefish are tender. Add water if the sauce becomes too dry. Check for salt, remove from the heat and put to one side.

Cook the macaroni for 10 minutes in 2 litres of boiling salted water with a dash of olive oil. When the pasta is *al dente*, drain and tip into a bowl. Stir in the cuttlefish and the sauce and serve immediately.

Ingredients (serves 4)

400 g macaroni
1 onion, finely chopped
2 cloves garlic, finely chopped
250 g cleaned sliced cuttlefish
2 tablespoons dry white wine

1 cup (250 ml) fried tomato
3 tablespoons olive oil
Salt
Pepper

Preparation

It should be said that this famous rice dish can be made with practically any ingredients you wish to include and, likewise, any of the ingredients below can be left out according to personal taste.

Heat the olive oil in a paella dish or large casserole and gently fry the chopped peppers, then remove them from the pan and put to one side. Use the same oil to sauté the chopped onion, then add the chopped garlic. Just before the onion is completely fried, add the peeled chopped tomatoes and continue cooking until the tomatoes are lightly fried and mixed in with the other ingredients.

Add the pork and chicken, both chopped into pieces. Season with salt and freshly ground pepper and fry until the meat is tender, then add the squid chopped into rings and cook for 5 more minutes.

Add the rice, stirring well so that the grains to do not stick, then pour in a litre of hot water so that the meat is almost covered (the water used to open the shellfish, previously strained, is ideal). Turn the heat up and boil for 5 minutes, then crush the saffron and add it to the pan, stirring it into the liquid. Check for salt, turn the heat down and simmer for 10 minutes (check the rice to see if more water is needed).

After this time, place the mussels and clams (boil for a few minutes in water to open the shells) on top, together with the two types of prawns (washed and raw), the strips of pepper and the peas. Simmer for 5 more minutes and remove from the heat.

It is always advisable to leave the paella to stand for around 5 minutes before serving.

PAELLA
PAELLA

Ingredients (serves 4)

400 g short grain rice	1 green pepper and 1/2 red
250 g pork loin	pepper
1 small chicken	2 medium-sized tomatoes
200 g squid	1 small onion
12 mussels	1 clove garlic
200 g clams	1 small tin peas
12 prawns	1/2 glass (100 ml) olive oil
4 small Dublin Bay prawns	Saffron, salt, pepper

Preparation

Wash the clams in cold water and place in a pan with a glass of water. Cook on a high heat until they open, then remove the pan from the heat and take the clams out using a slotted spoon. Remove and discard one half of their shells and place the clams in a casserole. Strain the water through a muslin and put to one side.

Chop the onion and garlic very finely and fry in a little olive oil. When they begin to brown, add a tablespoon of breadcrumbs and a few sprigs of very finely chopped parsley. Stir well and pour in the water from the clams, the white wine, the juice of the lemon and the chilli pepper.

Bring to the boil, then pour the sauce over the clams and cook gently for 5 or 6 minutes. Check for salt and serve piping hot in the same dish. The sauce should be quite thick (add more breadcrumbs if necessary).

ALMEJAS A LA MARINERA
CLAMS WITH GARLIC

Ingredients (serves 4)

1 kg clams	4 cloves garlic
1 glass (150 ml) white wine	1 red chilli pepper
Breadcrumbs	Parsley
1 lemon	Olive oil
1 large onion	Salt

Preparation

Cut the cod into thick pieces and leave to soak in water to remove all the salt. Then remove the scales and dry the fish thoroughly. Place in a casserole, cover with water and cook until froth begins to appear, then remove from the heat and rinse well.

Separate the layers of cod and remove the skin and bones, but do not discard. Chop the onion and garlic and fry gently so as they do not brown. When they are soft, add the breadcrumbs and stir well. Crush the skin and bones from the fish in a mortar and mix with half of the white wine. Blend the resulting mixture in a food processor with the rest of the wine and add to the onion. Sprinkle in the paprika and cook for a further 5 minutes.

In an ovenproof dish, place a layer of sauce, then a few pieces of sweet red pepper and a layer of cod. Then place another layer of sauce, another of peppers and one of cod, with a final topping of pepper strips. Bring to the boil, then remove from the heat, cover and place in the oven at a high temperature for around 20 minutes. Serve hot in the same dish.

BACALAO A LA RIOJANA
LA RIOJA-STYLE COD

Ingredients (serves 4)

500 g cod
1/2 glass (75 ml) white wine
1/2 tin sweet red peppers (*pimientos morrones*)
1 tablespoon breadcrumbs
2 onions
2 cloves garlic
1 tablespoon paprika
Olive oil

Preparation

The cod should be thin and flexible. The success of this dish depends on the quality of the fish. Cut the thinner part into squares and soak in water for 18 to 24 hours, depending on the thickness of the cod, changing the water two or three times.

With the cod desalted, remove the scales (taking care not to break the skin) and remove the bones. Place the cod pieces with the skin face down in a large earthenware casserole or several smaller ones so that the cod has plenty of room. Wash the dried red peppers, remove the seeds and soak in hot water.

Chop the onion into small pieces and fry in plenty of oil, together with the garlic cloves (left whole) and a sprig of parsley, stirring occasionally. Peel and chop the tomatoes and, when the onion is soft, add them to the pan with a teaspoon of sugar to remove the acidity and a piece of the chilli pepper.

Drain the dried red peppers and scrape out the flesh from the inside with a spoon. Add this to the pan. Crush the skins in a mortar with the cooked egg yolk and the almonds. Sprinkle the flour into the mixture and mix with a little water.

Pour the mixture into the pan and bring it all to the boil for a few minutes, then blend the sauce in a food processor, making sure that the sauce is smooth but thick. Pour over the cod pieces, sprinkle the breadcrumbs over the top and cook for 20 minutes on a low heat.

It is a good idea to shake the pan occasionally to make sure that the cod does not stick to the bottom and that the oil does not remain on top. When the fish is ready (there should still be plenty of sauce left), check for salt and serve in the same casserole.

BACALAO A LA VIZCAÍNA
BISCAY-STYLE COD

Ingredients (serves 4)

500 g cod	1/2 tablespoon flour
2 large onions	1 teaspoon sugar
2 cloves garlic	6 almonds
8 dried red peppers (*ñoras*)	1 red chilli pepper
1 kg tomatoes	Parsley
1 cooked egg yolk	Olive oil
2 tablespoons breadcrumbs	Salt

Preparation

Season the cod with a little salt. Chop the garlic and a sprig of parsley and fry them in a casserole with olive oil. When they begin to brown, add the cod fillets and a small glass (100 ml) of dry white wine.

In a separate pan, cook the clams in water until the shells open and then add them to the cod. Strain the water through a muslin, to catch any sand, and pour into the casserole.

Cook on a moderate heat for 10 to 15 minutes, depending on the thickness of the fillets, turning the fillets over once so that they cook on both sides. When ready, remove from the heat and allow to stand for 5 minutes before serving.

BACALAO FRESCO CON ALMEJAS
FRESH COD WITH CLAMS

Ingredients (serves 4)

500 g fresh cod fillets
12 clean clams
1 clove garlic
Dry white wine
Parsley
Olive oil
Pepper
Salt

Preparation

Peel and chop the onion, carrot, leek and garlic and fry in a casserole with 4 tablespoons of olive oil. Before they brown, add the bay leaves, a few sprigs of chopped parsley, a sprig of thyme, the white wine and the cleaned cockles.

Season with salt, cover the pan and cook on a high heat for 8 minutes until the cockles open their shells. Strain the liquid through a muslin, place the cockles on a large platter and serve with the sauce poured over the top.

BERBERECHOS AL VAPOR
STEAMED COCKLES

Ingredients (serves 4)

1.5 kg cockles	2 bay leaves
1 glass (150 ml) white wine	Parsley
2 leeks	Fresh thyme
1 carrot	Olive oil
1 large onion	Salt
1 clove garlic	

Preparation

Clean the bream and remove the scales. Make two or three incisions in the side of the fish to insert strips of pepper and slices of lemon. When this is done, place the fish in an elongated ovenproof dish or fish pan, season with salt and pour lemon juice, a dash of olive oil, the white wine and around 8 tablespoons of vinegar over the top.

Place the dish in the oven at a moderate temperature for 10 minutes. Meanwhile, chop a couple of sprigs of parsley and the garlic and mix with the breadcrumbs. Remove the fish from the oven, sprinkle the breadcrumb mixture over the fish and spoon any juices from the fish over the top.

Return to the oven and cook for a further 10 minutes, then carefully place them on a platter and decorate with slices of hard-boiled egg, chunks of lemon and parsley. Spoon the juices from the fish over the top.

Serve with mayonnaise in a separate bowl.

BESUGO AL LIMÓN
RED BREAM WITH LEMON

Ingredients (serves 6)

2 medium-sized red bream	2 tablespoons breadcrumbs
2 hard-boiled eggs	Vinegar
1/2 glass (75 ml) white wine	Mayonnaise
3 lemons	4 cloves garlic
2 sweet red peppers (*pimientos morrones*)	Parsley
	Olive oil
	Salt

Preparation

Remove the scales, open the fish up lengthways, remove the head and the backbone and wash in plenty of water. Peel the potatoes and cut into slices around half a centimetre thick, season with salt and parsley and place in an ovenproof dish.

Crush the garlic and a sprig of parsley and mix with the breadcrumbs, a dash of olive oil and a few drops of lemon juice. Soak the fish in the mixture, then place it opened up on top of the potatoes and pour three or four tablespoons of olive oil over the top. Place in a pre-heated oven at a medium to high temperature for 15 or 20 minutes. If you like the fish browned, place it under the grill for 5 minutes before serving.

BESUGO CON PATATAS
RED BREAM WITH POTATOES

Ingredients (serves 4)

1 red bream, weighing 1 kg
750 g potatoes
50 g breadcrumbs
1 lemon
2 cloves garlic
Olive oil
Parsley
Salt

Preparation

Slice the tuna into steaks, remove the skin, and season with salt. Coat in flour and fry in a little olive oil. When it is browned, place in a casserole. Strain the oil through a sieve to remove any burnt flour and use the oil to fry the chopped onion.

When the onion begins to brown, add to the tuna together with the peas. Crush the garlic in a mortar with a sprig of parsley and the paprika. Mix with the white wine and add to the fish.

Shake the casserole to mix everything together and check for salt. Cook on a low heat for 5 to 10 minutes until the tuna is cooked and serve in the same dish.

BONITO EN CAZUELA
TUNA CASSEROLE

Ingredients (serves 4)

1 kg tuna	1/2 teaspoon paprika
1 large onion	Flour
3 cloves garlic	Parsley
1 large tin peas	Olive oil
1/2 glass (75 ml) white wine	Salt

Preparation

Remove the skin and bones from the tuna and place in the blender to flake it into small pieces. Crush some garlic and parsley in a mortar and use to season the fish together with a pinch of salt. Finely chop the onion and fry in a little olive oil, then add to the tuna with a dash of white wine and one of the eggs, previously beaten. Mix well and press down to form a cake, which can then be placed on a clean, floured tea towel to make it easier to roll.

Use the two remaining eggs to make a French omelette and place it on top of the tuna, together with a few strips of pepper. Now roll it all up and place in an ovenproof dish or fish pan. Heat some olive oil in a frying pan and when hot, pour over the tuna. Place in the oven until it browns, then take it out, pour off the oil and leave to cool.

When it is completely cold, cut into slices and place in a casserole or serving dish, cover with the tomato sauce and heat in the oven for a few minutes before serving.

BONITO EN ROLLO
TUNA ROLL

Ingredients (serves 6)

1 kg tuna	1/2 onion
3 eggs	Garlic
2 tinned peppers	Parsley
Tomato sauce	Olive oil
Flour	Salt
White wine	

Preparation

Clean the mackerel, remove the heads and season with salt. Cover the bottom of an earthenware casserole or ovenproof dish with half of the onion and carrot. Place the mackerel on top, coat with white wine and cover with the rest of the onion and carrot, the clove of garlic and a tablespoon of chopped parsley.

Sprinkle a little salt and pepper over the top and cover to retain the steam. Cook on a low heat for 45 minutes. Shake the casserole a few times to make sure that the fish does not stick to the bottom and to mix all the ingredients together.

After 45 minutes, check to see if the mackerel and vegetables are cooked. When ready, remove the lid and place in the oven to reduce the sauce. Serve the mackerel in the same casserole, with a side dish of boiled potatoes.

CABALLAS ENCEBOLLADAS
MACKEREL WITH ONION

Ingredients (serves 4)

1 kg mackerel (3 or 4 fish)	Pepper
2 onions, chopped into rings	Parsley
1 clove garlic, crushed	Olive oil
1 carrot, sliced or julienne	Salt
1 small glass (100 ml) white wine	

Preparation

Clean the squid, removing the skin, the eyes and the ink sac (the ink is not required in this recipe). Cut the fins and the tentacles, cut into small pieces and mix them with the ham, also finely chopped.

Chop half the onion very finely. Heat 3 tablespoons of oil in a frying pan and sauté the onion gently. When it is soft, add the chopped ham and squid and fry for a few moments more, then remove from the pan, draining off as much oil as possible, and place in a bowl. Prepare the stuffing by chopping the hard-boiled egg, the olives, a clove of garlic and a sprig of parsley. Stir them into the bowl with the ham and squid pieces and use the mixture to stuff the squid, closing the opening with toothpicks.

Now heat a little oil in a casserole and brown the squid. Add the other half of the onion, also chopped, and fry gently.

Crush 3 cloves of garlic and a few sprigs of parsley, mix with a table-spoon of flour and a little white wine and add to the squid. Cover and cook for 40 minutes. Remove the squid from the pan and chop into slices. Blend the sauce in a food processor and pour over the squid slices. Serve hot with diced chips or as a cold dish.

CALAMAR RELLENO
STUFFED SQUID

Ingredients (serves 4)

1 large squid	Milk
50 g ham	1 onion
1 tablespoon breadcrumbs	Garlic
1 hard-boiled egg	Parsley
Flour	Olive oil
White wine	Salt
Potatoes	
Stuffed olives	

Preparation

Separate the heads of the squid from the tentacles, clean the insides, remove the skin and cut into rings 1 cm thick. Cut the fins into strips 5 cm long and place everything in a bowl with the bay leaf, the juice of the lemon and a small amount of olive oil. Leave to marinate for half an hour, turning occasionally.

Meanwhile, prepare the mixture for the batter. Separate the eggs and place the yolks in a bowl with the flour. Mix well and add the milk, 2 table-spoons of oil and a pinch of salt. Mix until smooth. Whip the egg whites until stiff and add to the mixture, stirring carefully until completely smooth and consistent.

Remove the squid rings from the marinade and season with salt. Dip them in the batter and fry in plenty of hot oil until they are golden brown and place on a serving dish. Serve piping hot with the sauce in a separate bowl.

CALAMARES A LA ROMANA
FRIED SQUID RINGS

Ingredients (serves 4)

4 medium-sized squid
2 eggs
1 small glass (150 ml) milk
100 g flour
1 lemon
Romesco sauce or mayonnaise
1 bay leaf
Olive oil
Salt

Preparation

Clean the fish, peel the prawns and season both with salt, but do not mix the two together. Finely chop the onion and fry in olive oil with the garlic and a few sprigs of chopped parsley. Before the onion browns, add a tablespoon of flour, stir in well and add the cider. Allow to boil for a few moments and check for salt.

In a large casserole, add a small amount of this sauce followed by a layer of fish and a layer of prawns, then another layer of sauce and so on until all the ingredients are used up. Heat the stew gently until the fish is cooked. If the stew is in danger of becoming too dry, pour in a mixture of cider and water. Serve in the same casserole.

CALDERETA DE PESCADOS Y MARISCOS
FISH AND SEAFOOD STEW

Ingredients (serves 6)

2 kg seafood (any type of prawn, rock lobster, etc.)
Several rock fish
1 glass (150 ml) cider (champagne or cava can be used)
Flour

1 large onion
3 cloves garlic
Parsley
Olive oil
Salt

Preparation

Wash and peel the prawns and put to one side. Finely chop the shallots and fry them in a frying pan with a tablespoon of butter and another of olive oil. When they begin to brown, add the shells of the prawns, the cava, a pinch of tarragon and salt to taste. Allow to boil for a few minutes and then cover and simmer on a low heat for 20 minutes.

Remove from the heat and blend the mixture in a food processor until the sauce is smooth and even, then strain through a sieve. Place the prawns in an ovenproof dish, cover with the sauce and place in a pre-heated oven at a medium temperature for 5 minutes.

When they are ready, serve the prawns in the same dish with the rice on the side.

CARABINEROS CON SALSA AL CAVA
LARGE PRAWNS WITH CAVA SAUCE

Ingredients (serves 4)

500 g large prawns (*carabineros*)
1/2 glass (100 ml) dry cava
3 shallots
White rice
Butter
Olive oil
Tarragon
Salt

Preparation

Clean the snails and place them in a pan with salted water, one chopped onion, a clove of garlic, a sprig of parsley and the bay leaf, and cook for 2 hours.

Meanwhile, finely chop the other onion and fry in olive oil. Slice the chorizo sausage and cut the ham into squares and add to the onion when it begins to brown, together with a tablespoon of breadcrumbs and cayenne pepper according to taste. Stir well, and remove from the heat. Crush a clove of garlic and a sprig of parsley, mix with a little white wine and add to the sauce. Add a little water and simmer for a few minutes.

When the snails are cooked, drain and tip into an earthenware casserole. Pour the sauce on top. Chop the hard-boiled eggs and add to the pan. Cook until the meat is tender and serve in the same dish.

CARACOLES A LA ESPAÑOLA
SPANISH-STYLE SNAILS

Ingredients (serves 4)

1 kg snails	Garlic
250 g minced pork	Cayenne pepper
150 g ham	Parsley
100 g chorizo sausage	1 bay leaf
2 hard-boiled eggs	Olive oil
1 glass (150 ml) white wine	Salt
Breadcrumbs	
2 onions	

Preparation

Females spider crabs are preferable for this dish, as they have the eggs, more meat and are generally tastier.

In a pan, bring enough salted water to cover the crabs to the boil, together with the bay leaf and a teaspoon of vinegar. Add the crabs and boil for 10 or 15 minutes, depending on the size of the crabs. Remove from the water and allow to cool, then open up the crabs carefully so they do not break. Scoop out all the flesh and the eggs and remove the flesh from the legs, making sure not to lose any of the juice released. Chop all the meat and eggs up together with the hard-boiled eggs, add the vinaigrette sauce, though not too much (the crab should be the dominant flavour), and serve by spooning the mixture into the cleaned crab shells.

CENTOLLOS CON HUEVOS COCIDOS
SPIDER CRAB WITH HARD-BOILED EGG

Ingredients (serves 4)

2 spider crabs
4 hard-boiled eggs
Vinaigrette sauce (olive oil, salt, carrot, onion, garlic, parsley and vinegar)
1 bay leaf
Vinegar
Salt

Preparation

Clean the cuttlefish, and put the ink sacs to one side (frozen ink sacs can be used). Cut the fins and tentacles into small pieces with scissors and put the bodies to one side.

Chop one of the onions and fry in a little olive oil. Crush a clove of garlic and a sprig of parsley in a mortar, mix with a little white wine and add to the frying pan when the onion becomes clear, together with the ham cut into small squares. Stir well and add the tentacles and fins, the paprika and a pinch of salt.

Mix everything together and remove from the heat to cool. Use the mixture to stuff the cuttlefish, making sure they are not overfilled to prevent them from bursting when cooking. Close the openings with toothpicks and coat the cuttlefish in flour before frying them quickly in hot olive oil. Remove them from the oil before they brown and place them in an earthenware casserole.

Use the same oil to fry the other chopped onion and 3 cloves of garlic. Before they brown, add a tablespoon of flour, the peeled and finely chopped tomatoes, salt to taste, the bay leaf and a pinch of nutmeg and pepper.

Stir the sauce and cook on a low heat for 10 minutes. Mix the breadcrumbs, previously soaked in water and then drained, with the ink, and add to the sauce. Stir well and cook for 10 more minutes, then blend the sauce in a food processor and pour over the cuttlefish. Cook for 35 minutes until tender and serve in the same dish.

CHIPIRONES AL ESTILO CANTÁBRICO
CANTABRIA-STYLE CUTTLEFISH

Ingredients (serves 6)

1.5 kg cutlefish	1/2 bay leaf
100 g ham	Nutmeg
4 soft medium-sized tomatoes	Parsley
White wine	Pepper
Breadcrumbs	1 tablespoon paprika
Flour	Olive oil
2 medium-sized onions	Salt
4 cloves garlic	

Preparation

Clean the fish and season with salt inside and out. Heat a little olive oil in a frying pan and fry the onion. When it begins to brown, add the sugar and a tablespoon of flour and stir continuously so that it toasts a little, making sure that it does not burn.

Add a glass (150 ml) of cider to the pan and allow to boil for a few minutes. Now pour half the sauce into a fish pan or long dish and place the bream on top. Cover with the rest of the sauce and dribble with cider. Place in a preheated oven at a medium to high temperature for 20 minutes.

From time to time, baste the fish with the sauce so that it does not dry out. When it is ready, serve immediately in the same dish. This recipe is also ideal for grouper fish.

CHOPA O SARGO A LA SIDRA
RED BREAM (SEA BREAM) WITH CIDER

Ingredients (serves 4)

1 red bream (800g)
1 bottle cider
2 large onions, chopped into thin slices
1 tablespoon sugar
Flour
Olive oil
Salt

Preparation

Remove the skin and bones from the hake, season with salt, dribble with olive oil and place in a fish pan or elongated ovenproof dish.

Crush the garlic and chop a sprig of parsley and fry in olive oil together with the onion. When it begins to brown, add the breadcrumbs, the diced tomato and salt and pepper to taste. Stir well and continue cooking for a few minutes on a high heat.

Add a small glass (100 ml) of dry white wine, stir well and simmer for a few minutes to reduce and thicken the sauce, then pour over the fish. Place the fish on the heat and bring the sauce to the boil.

Now place the dish in a pre-heated oven at a medium to high temperature and cook until the liquid from the fish has evaporated. Sprinkle chopped parsley over the top and serve in the same dish.

COLA DE MERLUZA CON TOMATE
TAIL OF HAKE WITH TOMATO

Ingredients (serves 4)

1 tail of hake, around 1 kg (fresh or frozen)	Dry white wine
	Parsley
500 g peeled soft tomatoes	Pepper
2 cloves garlic	Salt
1 chopped onion	
1 tablespoon breadcrumbs	
Olive oil	

Preparation

Peel and chop the potatoes into slices and boil in a pan with salted water, together with half an onion and the bay leaf. Halfway through the cooking process, add the fish steaks and continue cooking.

Crush the garlic slightly, but leave them whole, and fry them in hot olive oil until browned, then remove from the frying pan and sprinkle in a tablespoon of paprika, stirring well so that it does not burn, then add a teaspoon of vinegar.

When the fish and potatoes are ready, drain well and place on a serving dish with the sauce poured over the top. Serve immediately.

Ingredients (serves 4)

4 conger eel steaks (from the open part of the fish)
4 cloves garlic
1/2 onion
1 tablespoon paprika

4 potatoes
1 bay leaf
Vinegar
Olive oil
Salt

Preparation

Cut the conger eel (the piece should be from the open part of the fish) into six pieces and place in a bowl. Squeeze the juice of the lemon over the top and dribble with olive oil. Cut the bay leaf into four or five pieces and place over the fish to marinate for an hour.

Chop the onions, garlic and parsley very finely and fry gently in a casserole with olive oil. Peel and chop the tomatoes, remove the seeds and add to the casserole, seasoning with salt. Cook for around 20 minutes.

Add the fish and cook for a further 25 minutes on a low heat. Slice the eggs into three and use to garnish the dish, together with spoonfuls of garlic mayonnaise dotted around the casserole. Serve immediately.

CONGRIO
AL ESTILO DE TARRAGONA
TARRAGONA-STYLE CONGER EEL

Ingredients (serves 4)

1 kg conger eel	3 cloves garlic
3 hard-boiled eggs	1 bay leaf
200 ml garlic mayonnaise (*alioli*)	Parsley
1 lemon	Olive oil
300 g tomatoes	Salt
2 medium-sized onions	

Preparation

Clean and scale the fish and leave whole. Season with garlic, parsley and salt and put to one side. Chop the onion into rings and place in an oven-proof dish or fish pan greased with oil. Place the fish on top and pour the juice of the lemon over the top. Peel the potatoes, chop into thick slices and place around the fish, together with the sliced tomato. Sprinkle everything with salt and coat with plenty of oil. Place in the oven and cook at a medium temperature for about an hour.

Serve on a platter with the fish sitting on top of the vegetables. Garnish with lemon pieces and parsley.

DENTÓN AL ESTILO MARINERO
FISHERMAN'S DENTEX

Ingredients (serves 4)

1.5 kg dentex
500 g potatoes
1 lemon
2 tomatoes
1 onion
2 cloves garlic
Parsley
Olive oil
Salt

Preparation

Mix the salt with the egg yolks, moisten with water and mix to form a smooth paste. Leave to stand for a few minutes, then use the salt to cover the bottom of an elongated dish or fish pan. Clean the fish, season the inside with salt, sprinkle the herbs over the top and place in the dish. Add more moistened salt until the fish is completely covered. Place in a pre-heated oven at 200º C for 35 minutes.

After this time, remove the dish from the oven, take off the salt crust and serve with mayonnaise or hollandaise sauce. Other fish can also be prepared in the same way.

DORADA A LA SAL
SALT ROAST GILT-HEAD

Ingredients (serves 3)

1 gilt-head, around 750 g
1 egg yolk
Mixed herbs (parsley, dill, tarragon or basil)
1.5-2 kg cooking salt

Preparation

Wash the mussels and cook in a casserole with a little water until they open, then remove from the pan. Strain the resulting juice through a sieve and put to one side.

Wash the prawns and cook for 3 minutes in the stock, then remove and place in a casserole with a little olive oil and fry gently for 5 minutes. Then add the mussels and the chopped wild mushrooms. If they are tinned, soak in warm water and dry with a cloth before adding them to the prawns. Season with salt and cook for a further 5 minutes.

In a mortar, crush the garlic and mix with a tablespoon of olive oil and a tablespoon of very finely chopped parsley. Add this mixture to the prawns and stir well. Serve the prawns in the sauce in the same casserole.

LANGOSTINOS A LA MERIDIONAL
SOUTHERN-STYLE *LANGOSTINO* PRAWNS

Ingredients (serves 6)

1.5 kg *langostino* prawns
500 g mussels
100 g wild mushrooms
Thick stock
1 clove garlic
Parsley
Olive oil
Salt

Preparation

Clean the fish and remove the scales. Make a few incisions in the side of the fish and place in an oven-proof dish. Squeeze the juice of the lemon over the top and leave to stand for 15 minutes. Season with salt, dribble with olive oil and place in the oven for 15 minutes.

Chop the onion and garlic and fry in olive oil, stirring well so that they do not brown. Peel and chop the tomatoes and add to the frying pan together with the bay leaf. Stir carefully and simmer on a low heat.

Add the wine, season with salt and pepper and continue simmering gently. In a mortar, crush the hazelnuts and almonds to form a smooth paste. Mix with a little fish stock or hot water and add to the sauce.

Check for salt and cook for a few minutes more until the flavours mix and the ingredients are soft. Pour the mixture over the fish, cover so that it does not dry out and place in the oven again for 15 minutes. Place the fish on a platter, blend the sauce in a food processor, pour over the fish and serve.

LUBINA A LA MARINERA
FISHERMAN'S SEA-BASS

Ingredients (serves 4)

1.5 kg sea bass (from the tail)	50 g toasted almonds
250 g tomatoes	1 glass (150 ml) white wine
2 medium-sized onions	1/2 bay leaf
3 cloves garlic	Pepper
1 large lemon	Olive oil
50 g toasted hazelnuts	Salt

Preparation

Clean the pike fillets, season lightly with salt and put to one side for a few minutes. In a bowl, beat the egg together with the wine, breadcrumbs and crushed almonds. Heat the tomato juice in a saucepan and season with salt, pepper and the juice of the lemon. Stir into the egg mixture.

Heat a little olive oil in a frying pan and gently fry the pike fillets on both sides, then place on a dish and pour the sauce over the fish, sprinkling the pine kernels and pistachio nuts on top. Serve with the pasta cooked *al dente*.

LUCIO AL ESTILO MEDITERRÁNEO
MEDITERRANEAN-STYLE PIKE

Ingredients (serves 4)

700 g pike fillets
250 g pasta (spaghetti, tagliate-
   lle, etc.)
2 tablespoons pine kernels
2 tablespoons pistachio nuts
1/2 cup crushed almonds
1 egg

1 glass (150 ml) port or
   Sicilian wine
1/2 cup breadcrumbs
1 lemon
1 cup (250 ml) tomato juice
Pepper
Olive oil
Salt

Preparation

Clean the mussels well and place in a casserole with 300 ml of water, the bay leaf, one onion cut into rings and a pinch of salt. Cover and cook on a high heat for 10 minutes. Remove from the heat and discard the shells, placing the mussels in an earthenware casserole. Strain the liquid from the mussels through a muslin and put to one side.

Chop the other onion and the garlic very finely and fry in olive oil. Peel and chop the tomatoes and remove the seeds. When the onion begins to brown, add the paprika, the tomatoes, the liquid from the mussels, the chilli pepper, the breadcrumbs and the white wine. Cook on a high heat until the liquid is reduced by half.

Blend the sauce in a food processor and pour over the mussels in the earthenware casserole. Dice the hard-boiled eggs and sprinkle over the top. Cook for 10 minutes and serve piping hot in the same dish.

MEJILLONES A LA BUENA MUJER
MUSSELS WITH TOMATO AND HARD-BOILED EGG

Ingredients (serves 6)

3 kg mussels	3 cloves garlic
3 hard-boiled eggs	1/2 bay leaf
750 g tomatoes	1 teaspoon paprika
3 tablespoons breadcrumbs	1 red chilli pepper
1 glass (150 ml) white wine	Olive oil
2 medium-sized onions	Salt

Preparation

Clean the hake, squeeze the juice of the lemon over the top and put to one side for 10 minutes. Season with salt and coat in flour, then place in an ovenproof dish. Pour a little olive oil over the top and place in the oven until browned, basting the fish occasionally with its own juices.

Remove the oil from the dish and use to fry the chopped onion, garlic and a sprig of parsley, seasoning lightly with salt. When the onion softens, add the tomato and half a teaspoon of sugar to remove the acidity and fry together for a few minutes. Blend the sauce in a food processor and cook for a few more minutes until the sauce thickens.

Wash the clams, cook in a little water to open the shells and place in the ovenproof dish together with the drained peas. Pour the tomato sauce over the top. Place in the oven at a moderate temperature for around 10 minutes and serve.

MERLUZA CASERA
'HOME-MADE' HAKE

Ingredients (serves 6)

6 hake steaks (around 200g each)	1 lemon
12 clams	1/2 onion
250 g tinned peas	1 clove garlic
500 g tinned tomatoes	Parsley
1/2 teaspoon sugar	Olive oil
Flour	Salt

Preparation

Peel and chop the potatoes into slices and boil in a pan with salted water, together with half an onion and the bay leaf. Halfway through the cooking process, add the hake. When the fish and potatoes are ready, drain well and place on a serving dish, saving a glass of the resulting stock.

Crush the garlic slightly but leave them whole and fry them in hot olive oil until browned, then remove from the frying pan and sprinkle in a tablespoon of paprika (or cayenne pepper), stirring well so that it does not burn. Add the stock and continue stirring to mix everything together.

Pour the sauce over the fish and potatoes, shake the dish slightly to mix all the ingredients together and serve.

MERLUZA A LA GALLEGA
GALICIA-STYLE HAKE

Ingredients (serves 4)

4 hake steaks
4 potatoes
2 cloves garlic
1 onion
1 tablespoon paprika
1 bay leaf
Olive oil
Salt

Preparation

Clean the hake steaks, smother them in lemon juice and put to one side for a few minutes. Finely chop the onion and fry in olive oil. Crush a clove of garlic in a mortar with a sprig of parsley, the yolk of the hard-boiled egg, the flour and a dash of cider. Add this mixture to the onion, then add the almonds and season with salt. Allow the sauce to simmer for a few minutes, then blend it in a food processor.

Place half the sauce in the bottom of an earthenware or ovenproof dish, place the fish on top with the washed and rinsed clams, then add the rest of the sauce. Chop the pepper and place over the fish (more or less pepper can be used, or left out altogether). Pour over the brandy and the rest of the cider and simmer on a high heat for 15 minutes. Serve in the same casserole, with the finely chopped egg white sprinkled over the fish.

MERLUZA A LA SIDRA
HAKE IN CIDER

Ingredients (serves 6)

6 thick hake steaks
250 g clams
1 glass (150 ml) cider
1 tablespoon brandy
1 tablespoon crushed almonds
(optional)
1/2 tablespoon flour
1 hard-boiled egg

1 tinned pepper
1/2 lemon
1 onion
Garlic
Parsley
Olive oil
Salt

Preparation

Clean the hake pieces, sprinkle with lemon juice and season with crushed garlic and salt. Place in an earthenware casserole and put to one side.

Finely chop the onion and fry in a little olive oil. Add the flour, stirring carefully so that it does not burn, together with the peas. In a mortar, crush a clove of garlic with a sprig of parsley and mix with a dash of white wine. Add to the onion, together with a small amount of fish stock (or half a concentrated stock cube) and saffron and allow to cook for a few minutes. Clean the mussels and scatter them between the pieces of hake.

Peel and slice the potatoes, fry them in olive oil and add them to the fish. Pour the sauce over the top, cook on a high heat for 15 minutes and serve.

This dish can also be cooked in individual servings. Place a piece of hake, a few potatoes and mussels in each dish and divide the sauce between the six servings. Serve piping hot.

MERLUZA CON MEJILLONES
HAKE WITH MUSSELS

Ingredients (serves 6)

6 hake steaks	Fish stock
1 kg mussels	1 onion
1 small tin peas	Garlic
3 potatoes	Saffron
1/2 tablespoon flour	Parsley
1/2 lemon	Olive oil
White wine	Salt

Preparation

Clean the hake, squeeze the juice of the lemon over the top and put to one side. Fry the garlic in an earthenware casserole. When browned, remove and put to one side. Peel the potatoes, cut into thin slices and sauté in the same oil. Add the tablespoon of flour to thicken the sauce, the bay leaf and a little water. Cook the potatoes for a few minutes until soft, add the hake (seasoned with salt) and sprinkle 4 tablespoons of chopped parsley on top.

Crush the garlic in a mortar, mix with a little water and add to the sauce. Cook gently for 15 minutes, shaking the casserole so that neither the hake nor the sauce stick to the bottom. Serve immediately.

MERLUZA EN SALSA VERDE
HAKE IN GREEN SAUCE

Ingredients (serves 6)

6 hake steaks
3 medium-sized potatoes
1 tablespoon flour
1 lemon
4 cloves garlic
1/2 bay leaf
Parsley
Olive oil
Salt

Preparation

Heat a little olive oil in a casserole and fry the garlic, then remove and put to one side. Peel and chop the tomatoes and fry in the same oil with a sprig of parsley. When the tomato is almost fried, add the clean, salted hake and leave to cook.

In a mortar, crush the garlic, pine kernels and hazelnuts, together with the bread soaked in vinegar or white wine. Mix with a few tablespoons of stock or water and add to the hake. Cook for 3 or 4 minutes and serve straight away in the same casserole.

MERLUZA AL ESTILO ANDALUZ
ANDALUSIA-STYLE HAKE

Ingredients (serves 6)

6 thick hake steaks
12 hazelnuts
12 pine kernels
Bread for sops
3 tomatoes
Stock

Vinegar or white wine
2 cloves garlic
Parsley
Olive oil
Salt

Preparation

Open the hake on one side and remove the backbone carefully so as not to break it. Wash the fish well and remove some of the flesh to make room for the stuffing. Mix the mince with chopped garlic and parsley and fry in a little olive oil, then add a few chopped olives, ham and hard-boiled egg. Pour in a dash of white wine and add the flesh removed from the hake. Beat the remaining egg, stir it into the mixture and check for salt. Mix all the ingredients together, then stuff the fish with the mixture and sew up the opening or close it with toothpicks so that the stuffing does not spill out.

Cover the fish with a clean tea towel and fasten with twine. Place in a pan, cover with cold water and add the onion, a clove of garlic, a sprig of parsley, a piece of lemon and salt. Bring to the boil and simmer for 30 minutes, then remove from the pan, untie the tea towel and place the drained fish on a serving dish. Peel and dice the potatoes and boil them in cold salted water. When soft, drain and place on a serving dish. Do the same with the carrots and add them to the potatoes. Add the drained peas as well, together with a few chopped olives and cover with mayonnaise to form a salad.

Use this salad as a garnish for the fish, adding a few more chopped olives, the shredded lettuce, thin slices of tomato and the asparagus tips. Cover the fish with mayonnaise, tomato slices and olives and serve.

MERLUZA RELLENA
STUFFED HAKE

Ingredients (serves 6)

1 kg hake from the tail (or 1 large whiting)	250 g carrots
	1 lettuce
150 g minced beef	1 jar mayonnaise
50 g ham	Stoned olives
2 hard-boiled eggs	White wine
1 fresh egg	Lemon
500 g potatoes	1/2 onion
1 small tin peas	Garlic, Parsley, Salt
1 tin asparagus	Olive oil
250 g tomatoes	

Preparation

Clean the grouper, cut into steaks, season with salt and coat in flour. Fry the cloves of garlic in plenty of olive oil until brown, then remove and put to one side. Use the oil to fry the grouper until brown and place the steaks in an earthenware casserole.

Strain the oil through a sieve into a frying pan, sprinkle in a tablespoon of flour and add the fish stock (save a spoonful) and a little white wine. Crush the cloves of garlic in a mortar with a pinch of saffron and mix together with the spoonful of stock.

Add this mix to the sauce, bring to the boil and pour over the grouper. Place the casserole on the heat and cook slowly for 10 to 15 minutes, shaking the casserole from time to time. Remove from the heat, sprinkle with chopped parsley and serve.

MERO A LA VALENCIANA
VALENCIA-STYLE GROUPER FISH

Ingredients (serves 4)

1 kg grouper
1 cup (250 ml) fish stock
White wine
Flour
3 cloves garlic
Saffron
Parsley
Olive oil
Salt

Preparation

Clean the grouper, squeeze the juice of the lemon over the top and put to one side. Wash the clams and cook them in a pan on a medium to high heat. When they open up, take them out one by one and remove and discard the shells. Strain the liquid they give off through a sieve and put to one side.

When the fish is marinated, season with salt and coat in flour. Fry in hot oil until brown on both sides, then strain the oil into a casserole and fry the finely chopped onion and garlic. When they begin to brown, add the paprika and a tablespoon of flour. Stir well, pour in the white wine, check for salt and add the liquid from the clams. Bring to the boil and add the pieces of fish, the hard-boiled eggs (cut into 2 or 3 pieces) and the clams.

Add a small cup of hot water or fish stock and cook on a low heat for around 10 minutes. Place the pieces of grouper side by side on an oval dish, with the clams and pieces of egg on either side and the sauce poured over the top.

MERO CON ALMEJAS
GROUPER FISH WITH CLAMS

Ingredients (serves 6)

6 thick grouper steaks
500 g clams
3 hard-boiled eggs
1 glass (150 ml) white wine
3 tablespoons flour
1 lemon

1 onion
1 clove garlic
1 teaspoon paprika
Olive oil
Salt

Preparation

Mix together 2 tablespoons of chopped parsley, a pinch of oregano, the white wine, the juice of the lemon and salt and pepper to taste. Place the swordfish in a deep dish, cover with the mixture and leave to marinate for around an hour in a cool place.

Meanwhile, wash the asparagus, cut the stalks into pieces and put the tips to one side. Finely chop the onion and fry in a little olive oil until lightly browned, then add the asparagus and season with salt and pepper. Cook for 10 minutes. Fry the asparagus tips in hot olive oil and put to one side.

Cut six rectangles of tin foil and place a steak on each one. Cover each piece with the wine, parsley and lemon sauce and close the foil, sealing the fish. Place the packets in the oven and bake for 10 minutes, then remove from the oven and pour the juices from the fish into the asparagus sauce. Stir well and boil for a few moments.

Place the fish (removed from the foil) on a serving dish with a garnish of the fried asparagus tips. Pour the sauce over the fish and sprinkle chopped parsley over the top before serving.

PEZ ESPADA CON ESPÁRRAGOS
SWORDFISH WITH ASPARAGUS

Ingredients (serves 6)

6 swordfish steaks	Oregano
400 g green asparagus	Parsley
1 glass (150 ml) white wine	Pepper
1 lemon	Olive oil
1 medium-sized onion	Salt

Preparation

Empty out the octopus head, clean the whole octopus in plenty of water, then beat it with a wooden mallet to soften the flesh (this is not necessary with frozen octopus).

Place a pan with plenty of water to boil, together with the bay leaves. When it begins to boil, add the octopus, bring the water back to the boil and remove the octopus. Repeat this process two or three times, and finally leave the octopus to cook for around an hour, depending on the size of the octopus. Add salt 5 or 10 minutes before the end of the cooking time.

Cut the octopus into slices and season first with salt, then the cayenne and finally olive oil. Serve cold on a wooden plate.

Pulpo a la gallega can also be prepared in the following way: once it is cooked, slice and fry in olive oil and a touch of chopped garlic and red chilli pepper. Add a touch of salt, strain the oil through a sieve and pour over the top. Finally, sprinkle with the cayenne pepper.

Ideal served with boiled potatoes (*cachelos*).

PULPO A LA GALLEGA
GALICIA-STYLE OCTOPUS

Ingredients (serves 6)

1.5 kg octopus
3 or 4 bay leaves
75 g cayenne pepper
Olive oil
Salt

Preparation

Wipe both types of mushrooms clean and cut into slices. Finely chop the onion and garlic and fry in olive oil in a casserole until brown. Add the mushrooms and stir well. Now add the juice of one lemon, the wine, salt and pepper, and leave to simmer.

While the mushrooms are cooking, wash the fish, sprinkle with salt and squeeze the juice of the other lemon over the top. Add the fish to the casserole dish, together with the stock, and simmer for a further 10 minutes until all the stock has been reduced. Sprinkle with parsley and serve.

RAPE CON SETAS
MONKFISH WITH WILD MUSHROOMS

Ingredients (serves 6)

750 g wild mushrooms	1 glass (100 ml) dry sherry
200 g mushrooms	2 onions
6 fillets monkfish (salmon, sole or john dory can also be used)	2 cloves garlic
	Pepper
	Parsley
Fish stock	Olive oil
2 lemons	Salt

SALMÓN A LA ASTURIANA
ASTURIAS-STYLE SALMON

Preparation

Soak the *ñora* in water the day before. The salmon should be skinned, free from bones and cut into even pieces. Season with salt and pepper and put to one side. Finely chop the onion and garlic and fry in olive oil. Before they brown, add a tablespoon of flour and stir well. Slice the pepper, peel and chop two of the apples, peel the tomato, remove the seeds and chop into small pieces and add everything to the frying pan, along with the cider. Cook for around 10 minutes.

Coat the salmon pieces in olive oil and fry until lightly browned. Remove from the heat and place on a serving dish. Wash the clams thoroughly and cook in a saucepan with a little water until they open, then remove and add them to the dish. Strain the juice from the clams and add to the sauce while it is cooking, then blend the sauce in a food processor and pour over the salmon and clams. Peel the other two apples and cut into thin slices to decorate the dish and serve.

Ingredients (serves 6)

1.25 kg salmon	1 soft tomato
500 ml cider	1 onion
250 g clams	2 cloves garlic
Flour	Olive oil
4 apples	
1 sweet dried pepper (*ñora*)	

Preparation

Remove the innards and scales from the fish, clean and rinse well. Finely chop the onion and fry in olive oil together with the chopped parsley and half a teaspoon of salt. When the onion begins to brown, add the peeled and chopped tomatoes and continue frying for a few more minutes.

Chop the prawns into pieces, add to the frying pan and stir once or twice before adding the grated cheese. Stir well to mix all the ingredients together, then remove from the heat and use a spoon to stuff the fish with the mixture. Close the fish with toothpicks, season lightly with salt and dribble with hot oil and lemon juice.

Place the dish in the oven at a medium temperature for 30 minutes. Baste the fish with the sauce from time to time so that it does not dry out too much. When ready, remove from the oven and serve.

SALMONETES RELLENOS DE MARISCO
RED MULLET STUFFED WITH SEAFOOD

Ingredients (serves 4)

4 red mullets	75 g grated cheese
150 g peeled prawns (fresh or frozen)	1 tablespoon chopped parsley
	Lemon juice
1 small onion	Pepper
2 tomatoes	Olive oil
1/2 green pepper	Salt

Preparation

Clean the sardines, removing the scales, the head, the innards and the bones. Wash and rinse well inside and out and season with salt and the juice of one of the lemons. Coat them in olive oil, cover in breadcrumbs and place in a greased ovenproof dish. Sprinkle with chopped parsley and dribble with olive oil. Place in the oven at a medium temperature until the bread is lightly toasted and the fish cooked. Serve in the same dish with pieces of lemon.

SARDINAS AL HORNO
OVEN-BAKED SARDINES

Ingredients (serves 4)

2 dozen large sardines
Breadcrumbs
2 lemons
Parsley
Olive oil
Salt

Preparation

Remove the innards, the heads and the backbone from the fish, wash and rinse well, season with salt and pepper and put to one side. Soak the breadcrumbs in 3 tablespoons of vinegar. In a separate bowl, mix together the ham, onion and garlic, all finely chopped. Add the breadcrumbs, rinsed of vinegar, the egg and salt and pepper to taste.

Mix everything together to form a smooth paste and stuff the sardines with the mixture using a spoon. Close the sardines with toothpicks, then place them in a greased fish pan or similar recipient and spoon 6 tablespoons of oil over the top.

Place the dish in the oven for around 15 minutes. Check that the sardines cook evenly on all sides and baste with their own sauce from time to time. Sprinkle with chopped parsley before serving.

SARDINAS RELLENAS
STUFFED SARDINES

Ingredients (serves 4)

16 large sardines	Chopped parsley
100 g cooked ham	Pepper
1 egg	Vinegar
1 cup breadcrumbs	Olive oil
1 clove garlic	Salt
1 onion	

Preparation

Clean the trout, remove the bones and season with salt and pepper, then put to one side. In a bowl, soak the breadcrumbs in cold milk. Finely chop the garlic and parsley and fry in a little olive oil. Pour in 3 beaten eggs and stir until they set.

Remove the pan from the heat and add the fourth beaten egg, a little mustard, the juice of half a lemon, pepper, salt, nutmeg, the two hard-boiled eggs (chopped) and the drained breadcrumbs. Stir the mixture well and use to stuff the fish. Close the fish by sewing or with toothpicks, place in an ovenproof dish greased with butter and dribble plenty of oil and the juice of the lemons over the top. Place in the oven, pre-heated to 180° C, for approximately 35 minutes.

Meanwhile, chop the onion and fry in a little olive oil. Wash the peppers, cut into small pieces and add to the onion with a pinch of thyme and salt and pepper and cook for around 20 minutes. Then blend the sauce in a food processor and pour over the fish in a serving dish. Serve hot.

TRUCHA EN SALSA DE PIMIENTOS
TROUT IN PEPPER SAUCE

Ingredients (serves 6)

1 salmon trout weighing 1.5 kg	6 cloves garlic
4 red peppers	Mustard
2 hard-boiled eggs and 2	Nutmeg
fresh eggs	Parsley
1 cup (250 ml) milk	Pepper
100 g breadcrumbs	Thyme
3 lemons	Olive oil
Butter	Salt
1 large onion	

TRUCHAS CON JAMÓN
TROUT WITH HAM

Preparation

Remove the innards from the trout, clean and rinse and season with salt and pepper. Stuff each fish with a slice of ham and put to one side. Chop the onions and fry in a generous amount of hot oil. Add the trout when the onion begins to brown.

Fry the fish on one side until golden brown before turning them over, so that they do not break. When they are fried on both sides, place them on a serving dish, sprinkle with chopped parsley and serve with slices or chunks of lemon.

Ingredients (serves 4)

4 trout
4 slices ham
2 onions
1 lemon in slices
Olive oil
Salt and pepper
Parsley

Preparation

Clean the scallops thoroughly and boil until they open, then remove one half of the shell, take out the main body of the scallop and place in a sieve, straining the water. Put the coral, the reddish or orange-coloured part, to one side. With all the scallops in the sieve, submerge them twice in a pan of boiling water. Rinse and coat lightly in flour, then fry them in hot olive oil.

Once fried, place in a casserole and cover with the stock and the wine and cook slowly for five minutes. Then remove from the liquid and place on a dish, keeping them warm.

Strain the oil used to fry the scallops through a sieve and use to fry the chopped onion, garlic and a few sprigs of parsley. When the onion begins to brown, add the liquid set aside from the scallops and cook until it reduces. Now add the corals and blend the sauce in a food processor, adding cornflour if it is too thin.

Cover the scallops with this sauce and place in the oven at a medium temperature for five minutes and serve.

VIEIRAS A LA GALLEGA
GALICIA-STYLE SCALLOPS

Ingredients (serves 4)

4 scallops (coquilles St. Jacques)
1 glass (150 ml) dry white wine
250 ml fish stock
Flour
1 onion
4 cloves garlic
Parsley
Olive oil
Salt

Preparation

Cut the pork and ham into cubes. Clean the mushroom (either fresh or from a tin) and remove the seeds from the pepper. Chop both into chunks. Thread on to skewers, alternating pieces of ham, pepper, pork and mushroom.

When ready, put the kebabs in an ovenproof dish and brush with oil. Add salt and pepper. Cook them in the oven, occasionally adding white wine, water, or a mixture of both. Serve straight from the oven.

The kebabs can also be cooked on a griddle and are ideal served with a green salad or French fries.

BROCHETAS DE LOMO Y JAMÓN
PORK AND HAM BROCHETTES

Ingredients (serves 4)

500 g pork loin or sirloin
250 g piece of cured ham
500 g mushrooms
1 green or red pepper
White wine
Pepper
Olive oil
Salt

Preparation

Cut the kid or lamb into even-sized pieces and season with salt. Leave the liver whole. Fry the garlic cloves in olive oil and then remove.

Use the same oil to brown the meat and liver. Remove the liver when browned. Add the chopped onion to the meat, together with a spoonful of paprika, one bay leaf and the wine (if possible use a *pitarra* wine from Extremadura). Cook until the wine reduces, adding water every now and again, as the sauce should be quite light.

In a mortar, crush the garlic, the liver, a few pepper corns and the sweet red pepper, which should be roasted with a little olive oil and the skin removed, and form a paste with a small amount of water or stock. When the meat is tender, add the paste to the pan. Leave to cook a little longer, check for salt, then leave to stand for 2 or 3 minutes before serving.

CALDERETA EXTREMEÑA
EXTREMADURA-STYLE STEW

Ingredients (serves 6)

2 kg lamb or kid
1 sweet red pepper (*pimiento morrón*)
1 lamb or kid liver
Olive oil
1/2 bottle red wine

1 large onion
4 cloves garlic
1 bay leaf, black pepper, paprika
Salt

Preparation

Wash the tripe in plenty of water, with a handful of salt and vinegar. Rinse in two or three changes of water, then place in a casserole, cover with water and bring to the boil with a little salt and a bay leaf.

When the tripe is tender (between an hour and a half and two hours), drain off the water and allow the tripe to cool.

Follow exactly the same process for the leg, snout and trotter, but keep the cooking water.

Once the tripe is cold, cut into evenly sized pieces and add the meat from the snout, leg and trotter. Heat a few tablespoons of olive oil in a frying pan and fry the garlic and a slice of bread.

When they are golden brown, remove from the pan and put to one side. Cut the pork into small pieces and fry in the same oil. Chop the onions and ham, remove the skin from the chorizo and cut into pieces. Add to the pork when it begins to brown, together with a touch of red chilli pepper (optional) and a bay leaf.

Stir in a tablespoon of paprika over the top. In a mortar, crush the slice of fried bread, the garlic, a sprig of parsley and a glass of stock. Mix with the white wine and pour over the tripe.

Cook for a further 30 minutes, adding the stock from the snout, leg and trotter bit by bit so that the tripe is kept juicy. Check for salt, turn the heat up and boil for a few moments and serve.

CALLOS A LA CASERA
'HOME-MADE' TRIPE

Ingredients (serves 6)

2 kg tripe	2 onions
1 leg of beef	3 cloves garlic
1 beef snout	1 glass (150 ml) white wine
1 pig's trotter	1 glass (250 ml) stock
150 g ham	Bread
250 g fresh pork loin	1 bay leaf, paprika, parsley
200 g chorizo sausage	Olive oil, salt

CAPÓN ASADO RELLENO
STUFFED ROAST CAPON

Preparation

Clean the capon and dry thoroughly, then remove the drumsticks and the neck. Wash the inside with brandy and rub the outside with crushed garlic. Prepare the stuffing by mixing the ham, cut into small pieces, and the breadcrumbs, soaked in milk and then drained. Stuff the capon with the mixture and close the opening by sewing or with toothpicks. Place the rasher of *tocino* over the breast and truss the bird with twine to maintain the shape.

In a large casserole, heat a little olive oil and place the bird in the pan together with the coarsely chopped onion. Season to taste with salt and pepper, cover and cook on a low heat for half an hour. Then place in the oven, covered with greaseproof paper, and roast for around an hour.

Remove the paper, pour the glass of brandy and a small amount of water over the bird and return to the oven to brown on a high temperature for a few minutes. Serve ready-carved with the sauce on top and a lettuce salad.

Ingredients (serves 10)

1 large capon (3-4 kg)	Lettuce
250 g cured ham (*jamón serrano*)	1 onion
1 large, thin rasher salt pork (*tocino*)	2 cloves garlic
	Pepper
1 glass (100 ml) brandy	Olive oil
Breadcrumbs	Salt
Milk	

Preparation

Trim the meat of any fat or tendons, season with salt and pepper, roll in flour and brown on all sides in a casserole with olive oil.

Crush the garlic and a few sprigs of parsley in a mortar and mix with the juice of the lemon and the white wine. Add to the meat and cook on a low heat until tender, turning occasionally and adding cold water if the sauce becomes too dry.

When the meat is almost done, add the olives. Continue cooking until the beef is tender and remove from the heat. Carve the meat, then reform into its original shape and serve with the olives round the edge. Ideal served with a lettuce or endive salad.

CARNE ASADA CON ACEITUNAS
ROAST BEEF WITH OLIVES

Ingredients (serves 4)

1.25 kg piece of beef	2 cloves garlic
1 lemon	Parsley
1 cup of stoned olives	Pepper
Flour	Olive oil
1 small glass (100 ml) white wine	Salt

Preparation

Cut away any tough skin from the edges of the chops and, if they are thick, soften them a little with a mallet. Season them with salt and chopped garlic, coat them in flour and fry in hot oil. When they are brown on both sides, place them in an earthenware dish and cover them with white wine. Cover and cook on a low heat.

Use the oil to fry the onions and potatoes (as small as possible) until golden brown. Add them to the chops, together with the stock (either fresh or from a stock cube), check for salt and place in the oven for 15 or 20 minutes until the meat and potatoes are tender. Sprinkle with chopped parsley and serve.

CHULETAS A LA CASTELLANA
CASTILE-STYLE BEEF CHOPS

Ingredients (serves 6)

6 beef chops, 250 g each	24 small onions
24 small potatoes	2 cloves garlic
Flour	Parsley
1 glass (150 ml) white wine	Olive oil
1 cup (250 ml) stock	Salt

Preparation

Cut the venison into large pieces, season with salt and pepper and place in an earthenware casserole. Add the wine, the *aguardiente* (similar to brandy), the herbs according to taste and the grated nutmeg. Leave to marinate overnight.

Heat a little olive oil in a casserole and fry the ham. Remove the meat from the marinade and roll in flour. Place in the casserole with the ham and part of the marinade and mix well. Place the dish in a medium oven and cook for about an hour and a half, turning the meat occasionally and adding more liquid from the marinade as the sauce dries. Check for salt and pepper.

Serve hot with the sauce, with a side dish of chips or salad.

CIERVO AL AGUARDIENTE
VENISON WITH *AGUARDIENTE*

Ingredients (serves 6)

2 kg piece of venison
200 g cured ham (*jamón serrano*), with fat
1 glass (100 ml) *aguardiente*
1 glass (100 ml) white wine
Flour
Thyme

Parsley
1 bay leaf
Nutmeg
Pepper
Olive oil
Salt

Preparation

Wash the knuckles well, dry them thoroughly and place them in a pan with 2 litres of boiling water, salt and a pinch of pepper. Add the peeled onion, the bay leaf and the cloves and cook on a medium heat for an hour, spooning off the froth which appears.

Once the knuckles are cooked, take them out of the water and use a sharp knife to make incisions in the skin. Thread them onto the spit of the oven and grill them for an hour and a half. Serve them with a salad and a sauce of your choice. Pork knuckles are much tastier cooked on a charcoal grill.

CODILLOS DE CERDO AL ESPETO
SPIT-ROAST PORK KNUCKLES

Ingredients (serves 4)

2 pork knuckles, 1 kg each
1 onion
2 cloves
Pepper
1 bay leaf
Salt

Preparation

Clean the quails and season inside and out with salt and pepper. Wrap in the *tocino* slices, tie with twine and fry gently in an earthenware dish with olive oil. Brown the birds evenly, then add the wine and turn the heat up until the wine reduces. Add a small cup (150 ml) of stock and cook for a further 15 minutes.

Wash and peel the grapes and remove the pips, squashing the grapes slightly to collect some juice. When the quails are tender, untie them, remove the *tocino*, place them in a dish and keep them warm. With the sauce from the quails, add a tablespoon of flour and the juice from the grapes and cook on a low heat, stirring constantly. Add more stock if necessary. Finally, add the grapes. Pour the sauce over the quails and serve.

CODORNICES CON UVAS
QUAILS WITH GRAPES

Ingredients (serves 4)

12 quails
1 large bunch white grapes
12 slices of salt pork (*tocino*)
1 glass (150 ml) white wine
Stock

Flour
Pepper
Olive oil
Salt

Preparation

Wash the quails and remove the innards, then brown evenly all over in a frying pan with a little olive oil. Remove and place in a casserole.

Chop the onion and garlic and fry in the same oil, together with the bay leaf and the sprig of thyme. When the onions are soft, add to the quails, pour in the wine, stock and vinegar and season with a pinch of salt. Cook on a low heat for around half an hour.

Allow to cool and place in the fridge for 48 hours before serving.

CODORNICES EN ESCABECHE
MARINATED QUAILS

Ingredients (serves 6)

12 quails
500 ml white wine
1 glass (150 ml) vinegar
250 ml stock
1 medium-sized onion

6 cloves garlic
1 sprig thyme
1 bay leaf
Olive oil
Salt

Preparation

Clean the quails and rinse the insides with brandy, then season with salt and fry gently in olive oil over a low heat. When they are browned, remove from the frying pan and wrap each quail in a slice of ham.

Remove the seeds from the red peppers and cut around the stem as if to stuff them. Place a quail wrapped in ham inside each of the peppers and place them in an earthenware dish. Peel but do not chop the spring onions, peel and slice the carrots, the garlic and the tomatoes and add to the dish. Coat the peppers with the oil used to fry the quails and place in the oven for around half an hour.

Remove from the oven, sprinkle with flour, pour in the stock and wine and cook for a further 20 minutes on a low heat. Serve hot in the same dish.

CODORNICES EN PIMIENTOS
QUAILS IN RED PEPPERS

Ingredients (serves 6)

12 quails	1 glass (150 ml) white wine
12 large red peppers	Flour
12 slices of cured ham (*jamón serrano*)	Stock
	Garlic
6 tomatoes	12 spring onions
4 carrots	Olive oil
2 glasses (200 ml) brandy	Salt

Preparation

Place the almonds on an oven tray and toast them under the grill, moving them around so that they turn golden brown on all sides. When they are ready, remove from the grill and allow to cool.

Chop the dates into pieces and place them in a saucepan, together with the cinnamon, the rind and juice of one lemon and a glass (250 ml) of water. Cook until the dates are soft, then blend the ingredients in a food processor until smooth and put to one side.

Cut away any fat from the lamb chops, season with salt and pepper and fry in hot oil. When they are browned on both sides, remove from the heat and place them in an ovenproof dish. Pour the date sauce over the top and place in the oven for 15 minutes, shaking the dish from time to time so that the different flavours mix together.

Serve the lamb with the almonds sprinkled on top and decorate with pieces of lemon.

CORDERO CON DÁTILES
LAMB WITH DATES

Ingredients (serves 4)

450 g lamb chops	2 lemons
100 g stoned dates	Olive oil
15 g almonds	Pepper
1 teaspoon cinnamon	Salt

Preparation

Trim the meat of any fat and sprinkle with salt. In a mortar, crush the pepper corns (around 75 g) and use them to coat the steaks.

Heat a little olive oil in a frying pan and fry the steaks (allow around 4 minutes per side for a medium steak). When they are done, remove from the pan, but keep them warm.

In a separate frying pan, flambé the brandy, then add the cream. Bring to the boil for a few moments, pour over the meat and serve.

Entrecôte pepper steaks are ideal served with chips.

ENTRECOT A LA PIMIENTA
ENTRECÔTE PEPPER STEAK

Ingredients (serves 4)

4 entrecôte steaks, 300 g each
1 glass (100 ml) brandy
1/2 glass (150 ml) cream
Black pepper corns
1 small glass (100 ml) olive oil
Salt

Preparation

Clean the rooster, cut into even pieces and fry in olive oil. Chop or slice the onion and when the meat is browned, add to the pan. Stir well and sprinkle in a heaped tablespoon of flour. When the flour has been incorporated, add the brandy and red wine. Season with salt and pepper and add a sprig of thyme, the bay leaf and chopped parsley.

Crush the garlic in a mortar with a sprig of parsley and stir in a little water or stock. Add this mix to the rooster and cook until the meat is tender. Remove the pieces from the pan and place on a dish, blend the sauce in a food processor and spread over the meat. A seasonal salad makes an ideal accompaniment.

GALLO EN VINO TINTO
COQ AU VIN

Ingredients (serves 4)

1 rooster	2 cloves garlic
1 glass (100 ml) brandy	1 bay leaf, thyme, parsley
500 ml red wine	Pepper
Olive oil	Olive oil
Flour	Salt
2 onions	

Preparation

Trim the liver of any sinewy material, chop into pieces and rub with salt. Finely chop the onions, the garlic and a sprig of parsley and fry in olive oil with half a bay leaf and a touch of paprika. Season with salt and fry on a low heat until the onions are soft, then cover and keep warm.

Season the liver pieces with salt and fry in hot olive oil for five minutes. Remove from the heat, add to the onions and serve piping hot.

HÍGADO DE TERNERA ENCEBOLLADO
BEEF LIVER WITH ONION

Ingredients (serves 4)

750 g beef liver
2 large onions
4 cloves garlic
Parsley
1 bay leaf
Paprika
Olive oil
Salt

Preparation

Clean the meat (use loin if possible) and place in an earthenware casserole with the wine, a few tablespoons of olive oil, a pinch of salt, a few pepper corns, oregano, thyme and the crushed cloves of garlic. Place the casserole in a cool place and leave to stand for 48 hours, stirring occasionally with a wooden spoon.

When the meat is ready, remove from the marinade and place in a second casserole with the lard and the *tocino* chopped into small pieces. Brown the meat lightly on all sides, then add the coarsely chopped onion, a few sprigs of chopped parsley and the juices from the marinade. Cover and cook for at least an hour until the meat is tender. Add water while cooking if necessary.

Remove the meat and carve half way down. Blend the sauce in a food processor and pour over the meat. Serve with chips and a green salad.

JABALÍ AL ESTILO IBIAS
IBIAS-STYLE WILD BOAR

Ingredients (serves 6)

1.5 kg piece wild boar	Parsley
100 g salt pork (*tocino*)	Oregano
1 glass (150 ml) dry white wine	Thyme
50 g pork lard	Pepper
Potatoes	Olive oil
2 onions	Salt
1 head garlic	

Preparation

Cut the meat into large pieces and place in an earthenware dish. Boil a litre of water with one tablespoon of sugar and another of salt. Chop the leek, slice the carrots thinly and add both to the water, together with a few pepper corns and the herbs. Simmer for 15 minutes and allow to cool completely. Pour over the meat, adding half a glass of sherry, and leave to stand for 48 hours.

After this time, remove the meat from its marinade and rinse and dry with a tea towel. Heat the lard and olive oil in an earthenware dish and fry the ham, chopped into pieces. Then add the pieces of meat and the small onions, which should be peeled but left whole. Stir well and add the chopped onion and the leek and carrot from the marinade. Season with salt and pepper, add the rest of the sherry and cover, leaving the stew to simmer gently over a low heat.

Meanwhile, crush the garlic in a mortar with a few sprigs of parsley, mix with the juice of the orange and add to the stew. Clean and chop the mushrooms and stir them in, then continue cooking until the meat is tender. If the stew becomes too dry, add more liquid from the marinade.

Place the meat, with the sauce, in a serving dish and serve hot.

JABALÍ ESTOFADO
WILD BOAR STEW

Ingredients (serves 8)

2 kg boar meat	100 g pork lard
200 g cured ham (*jamón serrano*)	1 orange
2 carrots	Brown sugar
12 small onions	1 large onion
1 leek	2 cloves garlic
250 g mushrooms	1 bay leaf, thyme, parsley
1 glass (100 ml) dry sherry	Salt, pepper
1 small glass (100 ml) olive oil	

Preparation

Clean the hare and cut into pieces. Season with 3 cloves of crushed garlic and leave to sit for an hour.

Now place the hare in a casserole. Coarsely chop the onion, crush the remaining cloves of garlic, chop the tomatoes and add them all to the dish together with a sprig of thyme, the chilli pepper, the bay leaf, a tablespoon of vinegar and the wine. Add a pinch of salt and a generous amount of oil and cook with the lid on until the hare is half done. Peel the potatoes and chop into large pieces and add them to the dish. Check for salt and leave it to cook.

When the meat is tender, remove from the heat, leave to stand for a few minutes and serve hot in the same dish or in a shallow bowl.

LIEBRE ESTOFADA CON PATATAS
HARE AND POTATO STEW

Ingredients (serves 4)

1 hare	5 cloves garlic
3 medium-sized tomatoes	1 red chilli pepper
1 glass (150 ml) white wine	1/2 bay leaf
500 g potatoes	Thyme
Vinegar	Olive oil
1 onion	Salt

Preparation

Place the dried apricots, the prunes and the sugar in a saucepan, cover with water and cook until the fruit is soft, then remove from the pan and allow to cool, putting the sugared water to one side.

Trim the meat of any fat and make 4 cuts lengthways (or ask the butcher to do it for you), season with salt and pepper and smear with butter. Fill the cuts with the apricots and prunes and tie the meat up with twine so that the fruit does not escape. Place the meat in a casserole with a generous amount of hot oil.

Brown the meat on all sides and cook on a low heat, adding water and the liquid from the fruit occasionally so that it does not dry out. When the meat is tender, remove from the casserole and place on a chopping board to cool. If the remaining liquid is too thin, add a pinch of flour and cook for a few minutes until it thickens.

When the meat has cooled down, remove the twine and carve the meat into slices. Arrange them on a serving dish and pour the sauce over the top. Place in the oven for a few minutes to warm it up and serve.

LOMO DE CERDO CON CIRUELAS PASAS
PORK LOIN WITH PRUNES

Ingredients (serves 6)

1 kg piece pork loin	Flour
100 g stoned prunes	Pepper
100 g dried apricots	Thyme
50 g sugar	Olive oil
100 g butter	Salt

Preparation

Trim the pork of fat and fry in olive oil. Chop the onion and slice the carrots and add to the pan, together with the bay leaf and a pinch of salt. When the pork is browned, add a glass of white wine, cover and cook for around an hour and a half until the meat is tender.

Peel the apple and remove the core. Add the peel and the core (without the pips) to the pork. Cut the apple into even slices and place in an oven-proof dish. Add the rest of the wine, the sugar and the butter and cook in the oven until the apple is soft and golden brown.

When the pork is ready, remove it from the sauce, allow it to cool slightly and cut into slices. Thicken the sauce with flour, heating it briefly, then blend in a food processor. Serve the pork on a platter with the sauce on top and the apple slices on either side.

LOMO DE CERDO CON MANZANAS
PORK LOIN WITH APPLE

Ingredients (serves 4)

1 kg piece of pork loin	1/2 tablespoon flour
500 g apples	1 onion
2 carrots	1 bay leaf
250 ml white wine	Olive oil
Knob of butter	Salt
2 tablespoons sugar	

Preparation

Wash the sirloin and cut into six fillets. Melt the butter in a pan and fry the pork for 4 or 5 minutes on each side, season with salt and pepper and turn the heat right down.

Beat the egg yolks with a pinch of salt and pepper and dribble in olive oil, stirring vigorously until the yolks thicken. Stir in the juice and rind of the lemon. Serve the fillets on a platter, placing them in the shape of a fan and pour the sauce over the top.

MEDALLONES DE CERDO AL LIMÓN
PORK SIRLOIN WITH LEMON

Ingredients (serves 6)

600 g pork sirloin
1 lemon
3 egg yolks
Butter
White pepper
Olive oil
Salt

Preparation

Soak the sweetbreads in cold water, changing the water several times until they are completely free of blood. Rinse well and prick with a fork so that they do not pop open when cooking and place them in a saucepan with plenty of cold water. Bring to the boil, scoop off any froth and cook for 3 minutes before draining and rinsing them in cold water. Remove the skin and any suet, chop into pieces and put to one side.

Finely chop the onion and garlic and fry in a casserole with olive oil. Chop the pepper into strips and add to the casserole when the onion begins to brown. Fry for a few more minutes before adding the sweetbreads. Stir well, then add the boiling stock. Add salt and pepper to taste and cook for 45 minutes until the sweetbreads are tender.

Place the sweetbreads and the vegetables on a serving dish and keep warm. Mix the stock from the vegetables with 2 tablespoons of natural yoghurt, a tablespoon of chopped parsley and another of chopped spring onion. Bring to the boil and simmer for a few minutes, then pour the sauce over the sweetbreads and serve.

MOLLEJAS DE CORDERO CON PIMIENTOS

LAMB SWEETBREADS WITH GREEN PEPPER

Ingredients (serves 4)

450 g lamb sweetbreads	1/2 spring onion
2 green peppers	1 natural yoghurt
1 medium-sized onion	Parsley
1 clove garlic	Pepper
1 cup (250 ml) chicken stock	Olive oil
1/2 lemon	Salt

Preparation

Rinse the sweetbreads in cold water and put them to soak in water for two or three hours, changing the water at least twice.

Bring a pan of water to the boil and drop in the sweetbreads for 4 or 5 minutes, then remove from the pan and place them in another bowl of cold water.

When they have cooled, trim them of any skin or fat and dry them with a clean tea towel before slicing them into small fillets.

Heat a few tablespoons of olive oil in a casserole and sprinkle in two tablespoons of flour, then add the stock and salt. Bring to the boil, stirring constantly, and add the sweetbreads, the onion (in one piece) and half a sprig of parsley. Reduce the heat and simmer for 45 minutes.

After this time, remove the onion and parsley and add the mushrooms (if they are fresh they should be cooked first), together with the two egg yolks. Stir well and allow to boil for a few minutes before serving.

MOLLEJAS DE TERNERA CON CHAMPIÑONES
VEAL SWEETBREADS WITH MUSHROOMS

Ingredients (serves 4)

750 g veal sweetbreads	Olive oil
1 tin mushrooms or 500g fresh	Flour
1/2 onion	Parsley
2 egg yolks	Salt
500 ml stock	

Preparation

Season the drumsticks with salt and pepper and fry in olive oil until browned, then remove and put to one side. Chop the onion and fry in the same oil.

In a mortar, crush the garlic with the pine kernels and mix with the wine. When the onion is soft, return the turkey pieces to the pan, add the garlic, pine kernel and wine mixture and shake the pan vigorously to combine all the ingredients. Check for salt, cover and cook until the meat is tender, turning it at least once. Remove from the heat and leave to stand for five minutes before serving.

MUSLOS DE PAVO CON PIÑONES
TURKEY DRUMSTICKS WITH PINE KERNELS

Ingredients (serves 4)

4 turkey drumsticks
1 tablespoon pine kernels
1 glass (150 ml) dry white wine
1 onion
2 cloves garlic
Pepper
Olive oil
Salt

Preparation

Chop the herbs finely and put to one side. Place the meat, which should be off the bone, in a casserole dish, wrap in the bacon rashers and tie with twine. Add 2 tablespoons of vinegar, 3 of olive oil, half the red wine, the peeled clove of garlic, the slices of orange, the chopped onion, a few pepper corns, the chopped herbs and salt to taste. Leave the lamb to marinate for 24 hours, turning occasionally.

After this time, take out the lamb and fry in a little olive oil until evenly browned. Remove and place on a large plate.

Using the same oil, fry the onion and garlic from the marinade together with the chopped shallots. When they brown, add a tablespoon of flour, mix well and add the meat. Pour in the remaining wine, another tablespoon of vinegar and a glass of water, check for salt and bring to the boil slowly, then simmer on a low heat for an hour and a half. Blend the sauce in a food processor and serve separately from the meat.

PALETILLA DE CORDERO AL MONTERO
HUNTSMAN'S SHOULDER OF LAMB

Ingredients (serves 6)

1.5 kg shoulder of lamb	4 slices lemon
2 thin rashers bacon	2 onions
1 tablespoon flour	1 clove garlic
1 glass (150 ml) red wine	Pepper corns
3 tablespoons vinegar	Thyme, bay leaf, mint, parsley
Olive oil	Olive oil
2 shallots	Salt

Preparation

Clean the duck and remove the innards. Leave the bird whole. Stuff with the chopped ham and olives and close the opening by sewing or with toothpicks. Now roll the bird in flour and fry in hot oil until browned all over, then place in a casserole and cover with water.

Season with salt to taste, add the bay leaf, a few sprigs of parsley, the coarsely chopped onion and the strained oil. Cook until the bird is tender (this will depend on the quality of the duck). Add the brandy to the sauce and cook until it reduces.

Serve the duck ready carved, with the stuffing in the centre and the strained sauce on top. Garnish with boiled cabbage and a dressing of oil and freshly squeezed orange juice.

PATO RELLENO A LA VALENCIANA
VALENCIA-STYLE STUFFED DUCK

Ingredients (serves 6)

1 duck	Stoned olives
150 g ham	1 onion
1 glass (100 ml) brandy	1 bay leaf
Boiled cabbage	Parsley
Flour	Olive oil
Squeezed orange juice	Salt

PATO SILVESTRE AGRIDULCE
SWEET AND SOUR WILD DUCK

Preparation

The duck should be plucked and cleaned and the innards removed. Truss the bird with string to maintain its shape, sprinkle with salt and coat in olive oil, then place the bird in an oven-proof dish greased with olive oil. Peel and finely chop the onion and carrot and add to the dish.

Pre-heat the oven and cook the bird at a high temperature for around 2 hours or until the meat is tender, turning the duck occasionally and coating it gradually with the sherry.

When the duck has been evenly roasted, take it out of the oven and carve the meat by removing the legs and carving the breasts into thin slices. Place the meat in a pre-heated dish and keep warm.

With the juices from the roast, add a small glass of stock or water, 2 tablespoons of squeezed orange juice, a teaspoon of sugar and a few drops of vinegar. Season with salt and pepper, bring to the boil and simmer for a few minutes. Then blend the sauce in a food processor and, if it is too thin, thicken with some cornflour dissolved in water.

Finally, pour the sauce over the duck and serve piping hot. Slices of orange or pieces of fried bread make an excellent garnish.

Ingredients (serves 4)

1 duck	Vinegar
1 glass (100 ml) dry sherry	Sugar
1 small glass (75 ml) olive oil	1 onion
1 carrot	Pepper
1 orange	Salt
Stock	

PECHUGAS DE POLLO AL LIMÓN
CHICKEN BREASTS WITH LEMON

Preparation

Cut the breasts open and season with salt and a pinch of pepper. Gently heat a few tablespoons of olive oil in a casserole and fry the chicken on one side for 10 minutes. Crush the garlic and place it on top of the meat, then turn it over, cover the pan and cook for 5 minutes until the garlic is golden brown, then add the lemon juice with two or three tablespoons of water. Cover and cook for 3 or 4 more minutes (shaking the casserole from time to time) until the sauce reduces. Make sure the meat is cooked by pricking it with a fork and serve when the chicken is tender.

Decorate the plate with a few slices of lemon.

Ingredients (serves 4)

4 chicken breasts
1 lemon and the juice of another
1 teaspoon black pepper
Olive oil
Garlic
Salt

Preparation

Remove the skin of the chicken, trim off any fat and cut open the breasts lengthways, like a book. Fill each one with a slice of ham, close the breasts up again with toothpicks and season with salt and pepper. Put them in a bowl, add the juice of the 2 oranges and a sprig of chopped parsley and put to one side for around 2 hours.

Clean and slice the mushrooms and fry them in olive oil with the crushed garlic. Cook gently on a low heat until tender, then remove from the heat and put to one side.

Remove the chicken breasts from the orange juice, coat them in flour and fry them in hot olive oil until golden brown. Then place them in a casserole, pour the orange juice over the top and cook on a low heat for 20 minutes, shaking the pan from time to time so that the meat does not stick to the bottom.

Add the mushrooms and cook for 5 more minutes, then serve on a platter with the mushrooms round the edge and the sauce over the top.

PECHUGAS DE POLLO RELLENAS
STUFFED CHICKEN BREASTS

Ingredients (serves 6)

4 chicken breasts, boned	Flour
150 g fresh ham slices	Parsley
400 g mushrooms	Pepper
2 large oranges	Olive oil
3 cloves garlic	Salt

Preparation

Soak the beans overnight, then cook in cold water until tender, season with salt, turn up the heat to boil them for a few minutes and drain.

Clean the birds, cut into two and fry in a casserole with olive oil. Chop the onion, garlic, parsley, tomatoes and pepper and add to the partridge when it is nicely browned, together with the bay leaf, a touch of pepper and the vinegar.

Cover and cook on a moderate heat until the partridge is tender, then add the beans, mixing everything well by holding the dish and shaking vigorously, and cook for around 30 minutes.

Place the partridges in the middle of a serving dish with the beans around the edge and serve.

PERDICES CON ALUBIAS
PARTRIDGE WITH BEANS

Ingredients (serves 6)

3 partridges	2 cloves garlic
500 g beans	1/2 bay leaf
1 fresh pepper	Pepper
3 tomatoes	Parsley
4 tablespoons vinegar	Olive oil
1 onion	Salt

PERDICES EN ESCABECHE
MARINATED PARTRIDGE

Preparation

Clean and dry the birds thoroughly, season with salt and pepper and put to one side.

Thinly slice the garlic and onion and fry in a casserole with hot olive oil. Peel and slice the carrots and add them to the casserole when the onion begins to brown, together with the herbs, the bay leaves, the partridges and salt and pepper to taste. Stir well with a wooden spoon and add half a glass (75 ml) of dry white wine, 6 tablespoons of vinegar and the juice of the lemon.

Cover the casserole and cook on a low heat for an hour or until the partridges are tender. When they are ready, remove from the heat and allow to cool. As with all marinade dishes, serve the partridges cold. They are even tastier prepared a day in advance.

Ingredients (serves 4)

4 partridges	Dry white wine
4 carrots	Vinegar
1 lemon	2 bay leaves
1 large onion	Pepper
2 cloves garlic	Olive oil
1 teaspoon mixed herbs	Salt

Preparation

Trim the lamb of fat and cover with crushed garlic. Leave for an hour, then season with salt and spread a mixture of olive oil and pork lard over the lamb. Place on a baking tray and cook in the oven at a medium to high temperature. After an hour, pour the brandy over the top and cook for another hour, basting the meat occasionally with its own juices.

Serve in the same tray, or place on a warmed platter and carve at the table. Serve with a hearty lettuce or endive salad.

PIERNA DE CORDERO AL HORNO
ROAST LEG OF LAMB

Ingredients (serves 4)

1 leg of lamb weighing 1.5 kg
1 glass (100 ml) brandy
50 g pork lard
1 small glass (100 ml) olive oil
2 cloves garlic
Salt

Preparation

Soak the raisins in the rum. Squeeze the juice of the orange and the lemon and grate half of the orange rind into a food processor and blend.

Clean the guinea fowl and cut into quarters, then smother in the fruit juice. Cover with tin foil and place in the fridge for 2 hours, then grill at a medium temperature for 15 minutes together with the juices from the marinade. Turn over and cook on the other side for a further 10 minutes, then place in a hot serving dish.

Heat the rum and raisins in a pan and add the marinade juices, the tomato sauce, honey and cream. Stir well and whisk lightly, then continue cooking for a few more minutes. Pour the sauce over the guinea fowl.

Peel and parboil the potatoes, then sauté them in a frying pan with olive oil and serve together with the guinea fowl.

PINTADA AGRIDULCE
SWEET AND SOUR GUINEA FOWL

Ingredients (serves 6)

1.5 kg guinea fowl
250 g small potatoes
1 tablespoon tomato sauce
50 g raisins
2 tablespoons honey
Olive oil

1/2 glass (75 ml) rum
1 orange
1/2 lemon
1 small tub (125 ml) cream
Salt

POLLITOS AL ESTILO CANARIO
CANARY ISLES-STYLE CHICKEN

Preparation

Clean and dry the birds and chop into two, squashing them a little with a cleaver or large knife. In a food processor, blend the bananas, sugar, a dash of vinegar, a tablespoon of mustard and a pinch of salt and pepper to form a smooth cream.

Season the birds with salt and pepper to taste, dribble in olive oil and roast on the griddle for 10 minutes on each side, squeezing lemon juice over the top and adding more oil if necessary. When they are almost done, pour over the banana cream.

Serve with slices of tomato and the ham, roast on the griddle.

Ingredients (serves 4)

3 small chickens, (500-600 g each)	Ham slices
50 g sugar	Olive oil
3 bananas	Vinegar
1 lemon	Mustard
Tomatoes	Pepper
	Salt

POLLO AL CHILINDRÓN
CHICKEN WITH TOMATO AND PEPPERS

Preparation

Clean and dry the chicken, cut into pieces and place in an earthenware casserole with a few tablespoons of olive oil. Fry until lightly brown. Slice the ham into small pieces, finely chop the onion and add both to the chicken. Chop two of the peppers (roast the third), peel and chop the tomatoes and add them to the casserole.

Crush the garlic, a sprig of parsley and a few pepper corns and add to the chicken. Season with salt and cook on a low heat until the chicken is tender and the sauce has thickened.

Peel the roast pepper, remove the seeds and cut into strips. Place them over the chicken, cook for a few more minutes and serve hot in the same casserole. Mixed herbs can also be added to this dish.

Ingredients (serves 4)

1 chicken	4 cloves garlic
3 peppers	Parsley
3 tomatoes	Pepper
150 g cured ham with fat	Olive oil
1 small onion	Salt

Preparation

Clean the chicken and dry thoroughly. Chop the spring onion, cheese, apple and walnuts, and mix the last three ingredients together. Season the inside of the chicken with salt and pepper and stuff with the spring onion and the mixture. Close up the opening either by sewing or with toothpicks.

In a large casserole, heat a generous amount of oil and brown the chicken evenly all over. Remove from the pan and place on a plate.

Heat the brandy in the same casserole and flambé well, then return the chicken to the dish. Cover and cook gently for about an hour until the chicken is tender, adding a little water occasionally if necessary. Serve the chicken ready carved, with the sauce over the top.

POLLO RELLENO
STUFFED CHICKEN

Ingredients (serves 4)

1 chicken weighing 1.5 kg
100 g cream cheese
1 apple
25 g shelled walnuts
2 spring onions

1/2 glass (50 ml) brandy
Pepper
Olive oil
Salt

Preparation

Cut the lamb into even pieces, season with chopped garlic and leave for half an hour. Heat a little olive oil in a frying pan and brown the lamb, then remove and place in a casserole together with the sliced carrots.

Chop the onion and fry in the oil used to brown the meat. When the onion is browned, add to the casserole, together with a clove of garlic and a sprig of parsley crushed in a mortar and mixed with the white wine. Cover and cook on a medium heat.

Peel the potatoes and season with garlic. Sauté them in oil, then add to the meat. In the same frying pan used for the potatoes, sprinkle in the flour and stir until it turns golden brown, add some water and allow to cook for a few minutes. Add this to the pan, cover with water and cook until the lamb is tender. Serve hot.

RAGÚ DE CORDERO
LAMB RAGOUT

Ingredients (serves 4)

1 kg lamb	Garlic
1.5 kg small potatoes	Parsley
250 g carrots	1/2 bay leaf
1 glass (150 ml) white wine	Olive oil
1 tablespoon flour	Salt
1 onion	

Preparation

Cut the meat into even pieces, season with salt and garlic and put to one side for 15 minutes. Heat a little olive oil in a casserole and brown the meat on all sides, then add the chopped onion and garlic, a sprig of chopped parsley, the tomato, the bay leaf, half a glass (75 ml) of white wine and the peeled and chopped carrots. Cook on a low heat, adding a chopped pepper halfway through the cooking process.

When the beef is almost tender, rub the potatoes with garlic, fry briefly in olive oil and add them to the stew, together with the peas (previously cooked if fresh and drained if tinned). Cover with water, check for salt and cook gently until all the ingredients are tender. Serve with strips of pepper.

RAGÚ DE TERNERA
BEEF RAGOUT

Ingredients (serves 4 or 5)

750 g beef	1/2 onion
1 tin tomatoes	Garlic
1 small tin peppers	Parsley
250 g carrots	1 bay leaf
250 g peas	Olive oil
500 g potatoes	Salt
White wine	

Preparation

The best kidneys are from veal or lamb, and they should be extremely fresh. Trim them of any skin and sinewy tissue, open them lengthways to remove the suet and cut into thin slices. Place them in a bowl covered with water and vinegar for 45 minutes.

Rinse and dry them well, season with crushed garlic and half the sherry and put to one side for an hour.

Chop the onion and half a tablespoon of parsley and fry in olive oil until the onion is soft.

Remove the kidneys from their marinade, season with salt and add to the frying pan. Stir well and cook for 8 minutes, then add the rest of the sherry and a teaspoon of flour. Cook for a further 5 minutes and serve piping hot.

RIÑONES AL JEREZ
VEAL KIDNEYS IN SHERRY

Ingredients (serves 6)

3 veal kidneys
1 glass (100 ml) dry sherry
1 onion
2 cloves garlic
Parsley
Flour
Olive oil
Salt

Preparation

The best kidneys are from veal or lamb, and they should be extremely fresh. Trim them of any skin and sinewy tissue, open them lengthways to remove the suet and cut into thin slices.

Soak them in a covered bowl with water and vinegar for 45 minutes, then rinse well, season with salt and pepper and fry in hot olive oil.

After a few minutes, mix the flour with the white wine and add to the pan, cover and cook until the kidneys are tender. Place on a platter with chopped parsley sprinkled over the top. Ideal served with rice or chips.

RIÑONES DE TERNERA A LA CASERA
'HOME-MADE' VEAL KIDNEYS

Ingredients (serves 4)

2 veal kidneys
1 glass (150 ml) dry white wine
1 tablespoon flour
2 tablespoons vinegar
Parsley
Black pepper
Olive oil
Salt

Preparation

Heat the cheese, the cream and a dash of cider in a saucepan, stirring all the time until smooth. Smear the fillets in oil and fry in a dry frying pan or in a hot griddle until brown on both sides.

When they are cooked, place them on a serving dish, pour the cheese sauce over the top and serve.

SOLOMILLO AL QUESO CABRALES
BEEF SIRLOIN WITH CABRALES CHEESE

Ingredients (serves 4)

4 thick sirloin fillets
50 g Cabrales cheese
1 glass (125 ml) cream
Cider
Olive oil
Salt

Preparation

In a bowl, mix together the flour, enough salt to completely cover the meat (1-1.5 kg), 4 egg whites and a small amount of water. Mix well to form a stiff paste and leave to stand for 2 hours.

Meanwhile, brown the sirloin in a frying pan with olive oil. Place half the salt mixture in an ovenproof dish, put the meat on top and then cover with the rest of the salt, pressing down so that the coating sticks to the meat. Preheat the oven to 220° C and cook for around 15 minutes until the coating begins to crack.

Prepare the sauce by mixing the mustard with the cheese. Finely chop the onion and fry in olive oil until it becomes clear and pour in the cream. Simmer for a couple of minutes and add the cheese and mustard. Cook for a few moments more but do not allow it to boil. The sauce should be served piping hot.

When the meat is ready, remove from the oven, cover with a cloth and remove the salt crust using a pestle. Place the meat on a serving dish, carve into thin slices and serve with the sauce in a separate bowl.

SOLOMILLO DE AÑOJO EN COSTRA

YEARLING SIRLOIN ROAST IN SALT CRUST

Ingredients (serves 6)

1.25 kg yearling sirloin
700 g flour
4 eggs
50 g cream
75 g fresh cheese (*queso fresco*)
2 tablespoons mustard
1 small onion
Olive oil
Cooking salt

Preparation

Make a few cuts in the meat with a sharp knife and add the cloves of garlic chopped in two, then smother the meat with mustard.

Place the sirloin in a casserole with the wine and cook on a moderate heat, stirring occasionally and seasoning with salt and pepper.

Meanwhile, peel and chop the onions and mix them with the basil. Add them to the meat after 15 minutes and continue cooking for an hour, turning the meat so that it is always covered with onions. Serve in slices with the mustard of your choice.

SOLOMILLO DE VACA A LA MOSTAZA
BEEF SIRLOIN WITH MUSTARD

Ingredients (serves 4)

1 kg beef sirloin
1 glass (150 ml) white wine
8 small onions
Mustard (any type)
6 cloves garlic
Pepper
Basil
Salt

SOLOMILLOS DE CERDO RELLENOS
STUFFED PORK SIRLOIN

Preparation

Ask the butcher to open up the sirloins lengthways, without slicing them in two. Crush the cheese with a fork to form a smooth cream, then add the peeled and chopped walnuts and mix well. Fill the sirloins with the mixture and tie them up with twine. Season with salt to taste and brown them in a frying pan with olive oil.

Once browned, place them in an ovenproof dish. Chop the onion and fry in the same oil used for the meat, then add flour, the stock and the white wine. Cover the meat with this sauce and place in the oven at a high temperature until they are tender and serve piping hot.

Ingredients (serves 4 or 5)

3 pork sirloins (1 kg)
100 g walnuts
150 g Roquefort or any other blue cheese
1 glass (200 ml) stock
Flour
Dry white wine
1 onion
Olive oil
Salt

Preparation

Trim the beef of any fat and nerves, cut into 5 cm cubes and season with salt and pepper. Finely chop the garlic, onion and a sprig of parsley and fry in a casserole with a generous amount of hot olive oil. When they begin to brown, add the meat and stir well.

Peel and slice the carrots, chop the mushrooms into slices and add to the meat together with the bay leaf and a teaspoon of thyme. Stir well and cook for 15 minutes before adding the stock. Cover and cook for a further 30 minutes.

In a bowl, mix the cream, the egg yolks, the cornflour and a pinch of nutmeg. Pour the mixture into the stew and cook for another 15 minutes. Stir the stew occasionally and shake the pan so that the sauce does not stick to the bottom. When the beef is tender, serve on a platter with lemon juice squeezed over the top.

TERNERA ESTOFADA
BEEF STEW

Ingredients (serves 5 or 6)

1 kg beef	Cornflour
250 g mushrooms	Thyme
1 onion	1 bay leaf
1 clove garlic	Lemon juice
2 carrots	Nutmeg
3 egg yolks	Pepper
500 ml stock (fresh or stock cubes)	Olive oil
1 glass (125 ml) cream	Salt

Preparation

Trim the meat of any fat and nerves and cut into even-sized cubes. Season with salt and pepper. Brown the meat in hot olive oil, then remove the meat and keep in a warm place. Finely chop the garlic and onion, cut the peppers into strips and fry in the same oil.

When the vegetables are well cooked, add the meat to the pan again, pour in the sherry and check for salt. Cover and cook for 45 minutes. Check if the meat is tender (leave it to cook longer if necessary), then remove from the heat, stir in the yoghurt and serve.

TERNERA PRIMAVERA
SPRING BEEF

Ingredients (serves 4)

500 g beef
1 small onion
1 clove garlic
4 thin green peppers for frying
1 glass (100 ml) sherry or dry
  white wine

2 tablespoons natural yoghurt
Pepper
Olive oil
Salt

INDEX

SOUPS, PURÉES AND APPETISERS

VEGETABLES AND PULSES

EGGS AND MUSHROOMS

RICE AND PASTA

FISH AND SEAFOOD

MEAT, POULTRY AND GAME